# Making Music for Folk Harp

By Susan Raimond

Online Audio www.melbay.com/96704BCDEB

## Audio Contents

| | | | | | |
|---|---|---|---|---|---|
| 1 | Intro [:20] | 12 | Flow Gently, Sweet Afton [1:06] | 23 | Brother John [1:18] |
| 2 | Drone/Octave/Split Octave [1:50] | 13 | The Grenadier and the Lady [1:18] | 24 | Music Alone Shall Live [1:35] |
| 3 | Triads [2:20] | 14 | On Top of Old Smoky [1:06] | 25 | Dona Nobis Pacem [2:54] |
| 4 | Left Hand Sounds [5:26] | 15 | Star of the County Down [1:30] | 26 | Shalom Chaverim [1:17] |
| 5 | Minuet in G [1:01] | 16 | The Sally Gardens [1:30] | 27 | Tanz [1:38] |
| 6 | Amazing Grace [1:53] | 17 | Simple Gifts [1:07] | 28 | William's Lullaby [2:19] |
| 7 | All Through the Night [1:25] | 18 | When the Saints Go Marching In [:43] | 29 | Gentry's Gait [2:06] |
| 8 | The Christ Child's Lullaby [1:15] | 19 | Jingle Bells [1:10] | 30 | Matilija [2:16] |
| 9 | Skye Boat Song [1:35] | 20 | The Ash Grove [1:31] | 31 | Aliso [3:01] |
| 10 | Greensleeves [1:57] | 21 | Jacob's Ladder [:59] | | |
| 11 | Brian Boru's March [2:22] | 22 | White Coral Bells [1:26] | | |

Raimond Harps and Lionwood Harps were used on the recording.

1 2 3 4 5 6 7 8 9 0



***Visit us on the Web at http://www.melbay.com — E-mail us at email@melbay.com***

# *Making Music: Contents*

## LEFT-HAND TECHNIQUES



## SIMPLE TUNES



## ROUNDS



## SOLOS

This book is a great starting place for beginners – and teachers – who want immediate results. The melodies are easily recognized and simple to play.

The suggested left-hand accompaniments are illustrated below.

## Drone

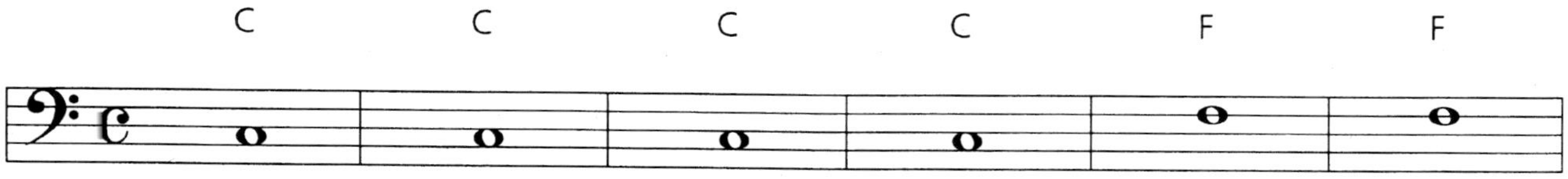


A sustained sound, usually of one pitch. Drone on the note indicated above the melody line.

## Octave

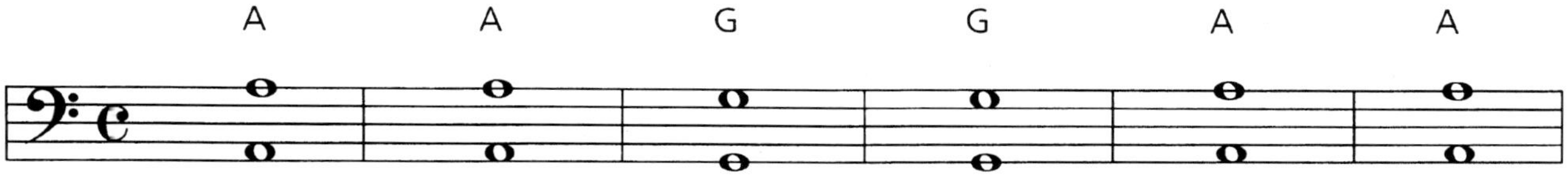


Two tones at an interval an octave apart.
Play the octave on the notes indicated above the melody line.

## Split Octave

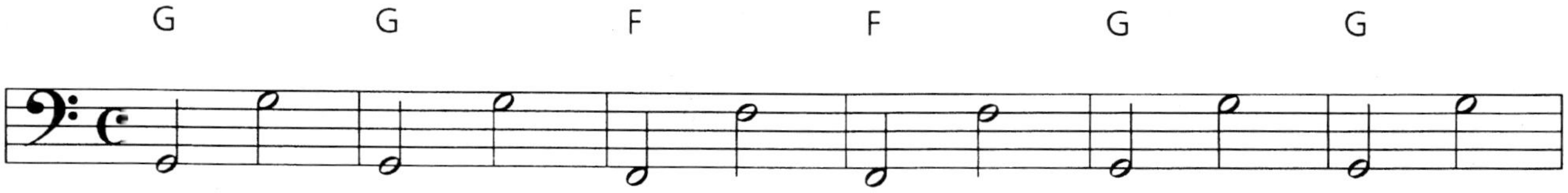


Two tones at an interval an octave apart.
Play the octave on the notes indicated above the melody line, with the lower note preceding the upper note.

## Triad

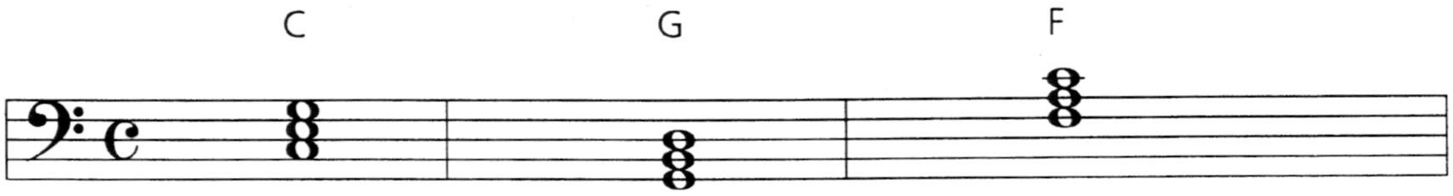


C - E - F
1 - 3 - 5

G - B - D
1 - 3 - 5

F - A - C
1 - 3 - 5

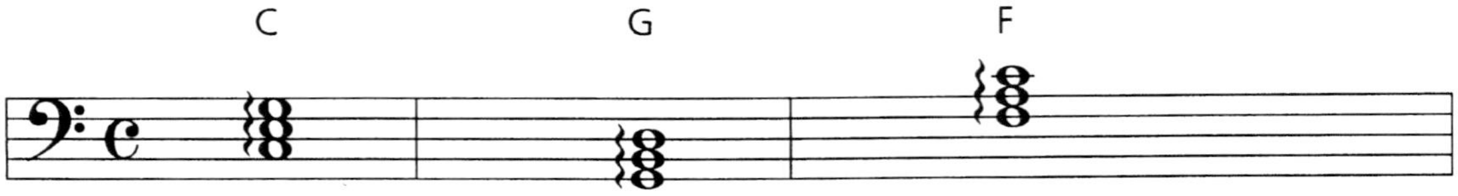


C - E - G
1 - 3 - 5

G - B - D
1 - 3 - 5

F - A - C
1 - 3 - 5

A chord of three tones plucked together or rolled (⌇).
Play the triad as 1-3-5 with 1 being the note written above the melody line.

## 1 - 5 - 8

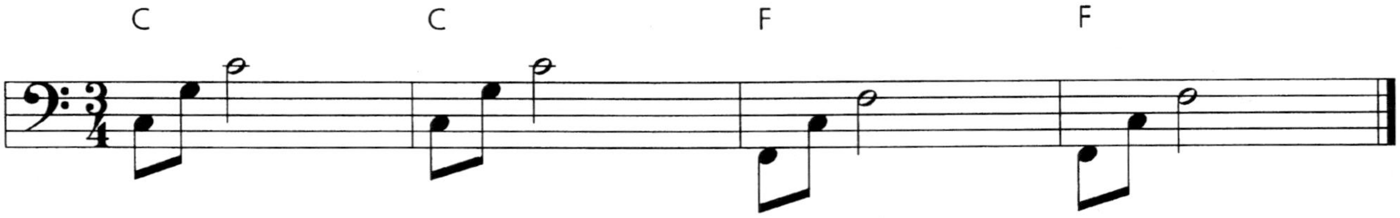


C - G - C
1 - 5 - 8

C - G - C
1 - 5 - 8

F - C - F
1 - 5 - 8

F - C - F
1 - 5 - 8

An octave with a fifth added.
Play beginning with the note written above the melody line as 1.

## 1 - 5 - 8 - 5 - 10 (Roving thumb)

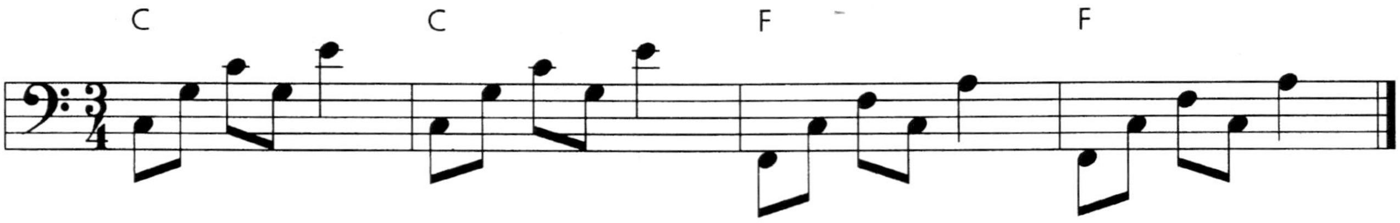


C - G - C - G - E
1 - 5 - 8 - 5 - 10

F - C - F - C - A
1 - 5 - 8 - 5 - 10

Use the 5 as an anchor – "roving thumb" plays the tenth note.
Play beginning with the note written above the melody line as 1.

# Left-Hand Accompaniments for the Harp

"WALTZ" TIME
APPROPRIATE WHEN
3/4 SIGNATURE APPEARS

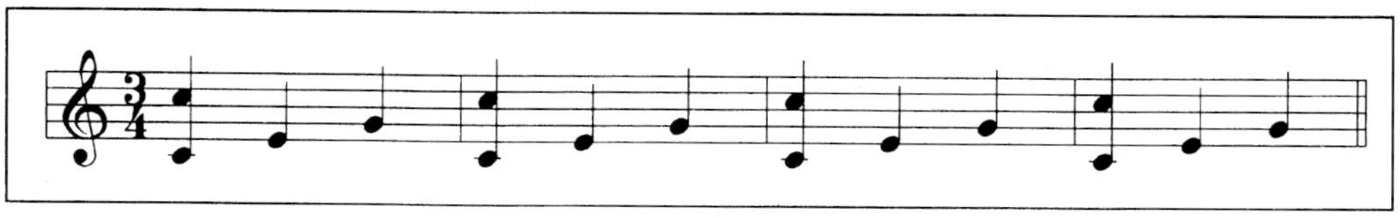

"MARCH" TIME
EASILY ACCOMPLISHED BY
PLAYING THE OCTAVE (FINGERS
1 & 4) FOLLOWED BY A THIRD
(FINGERS 2 & 3)

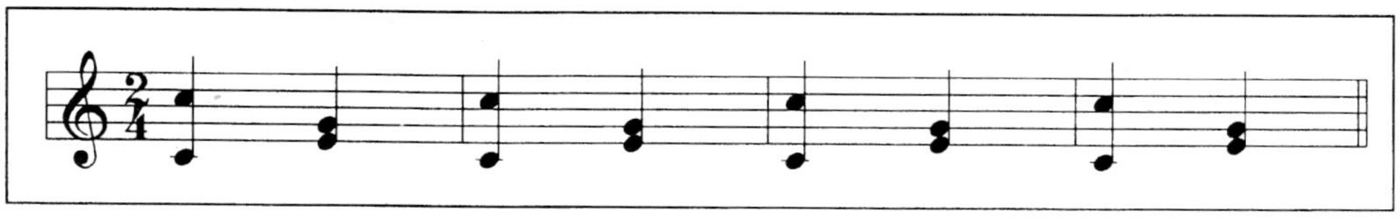

A TYPICAL VENEZUELAN
ACCOMPANIMENT

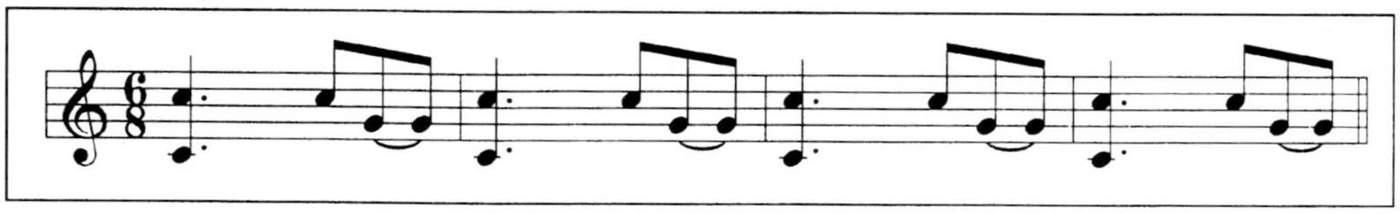

1 - 5 - 8 - 5 - 10

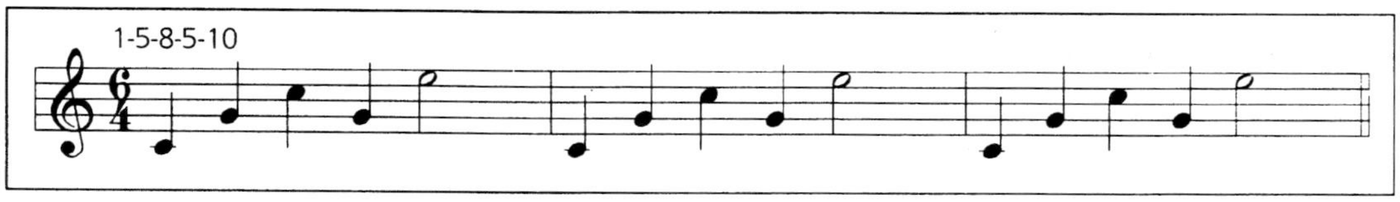


TRIADS

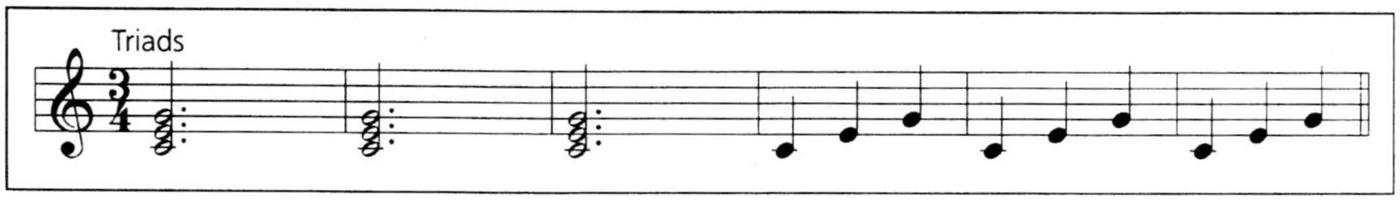


DRONE

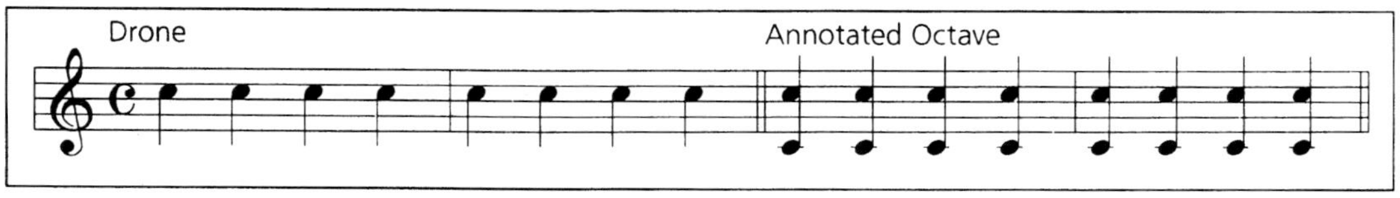


SPLIT DRONE

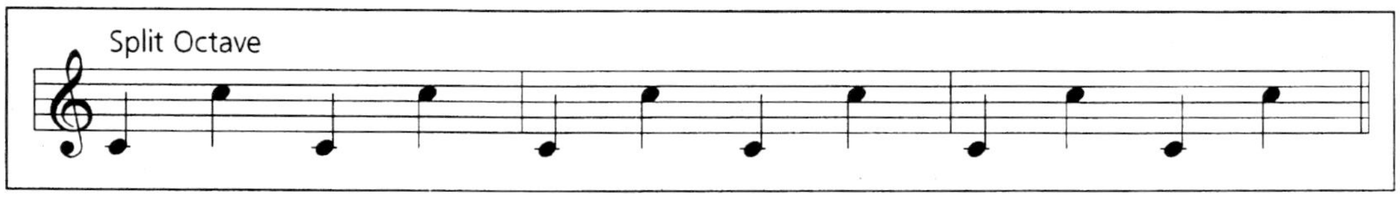


USE WHEN YOU ARPEGGIATE
FINGERING 4 - 2 - 1 (CROSS
UNDER) 3 - 2 - 1

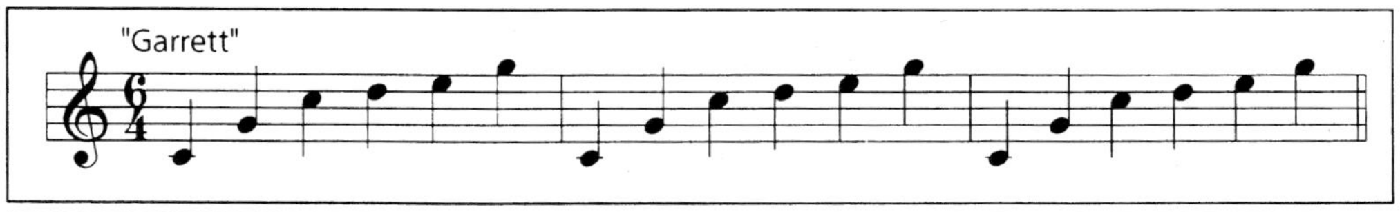


GARRETT PLUS SIMPLY ALLOWS THE LAST THREE NOTES OF THE GARRETT TO BE REPEATED COMING DOWN THE SCALE. PICTURE A WAVE BUILDING AND THEN CRESTING AND RELAXING. A VERY SIMPLE YET DRAMATIC LEFT-HAND TECHNIQUE!

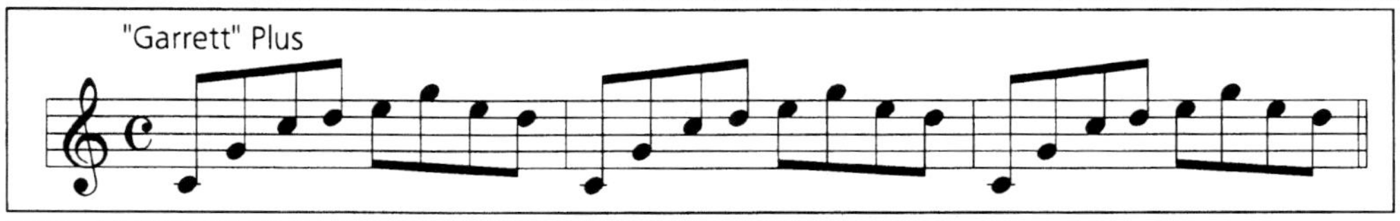


ROVING THUMB

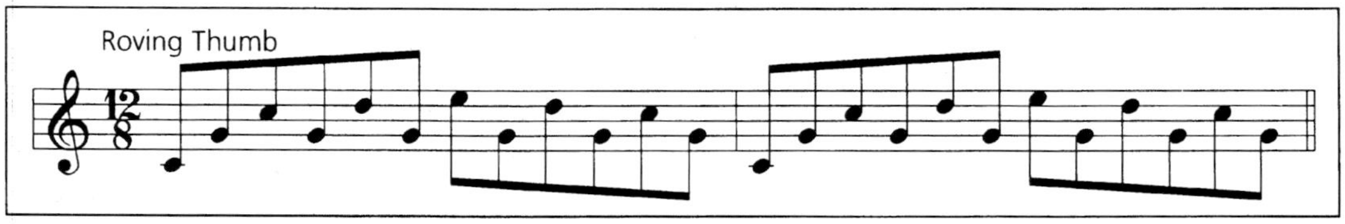


GAIT

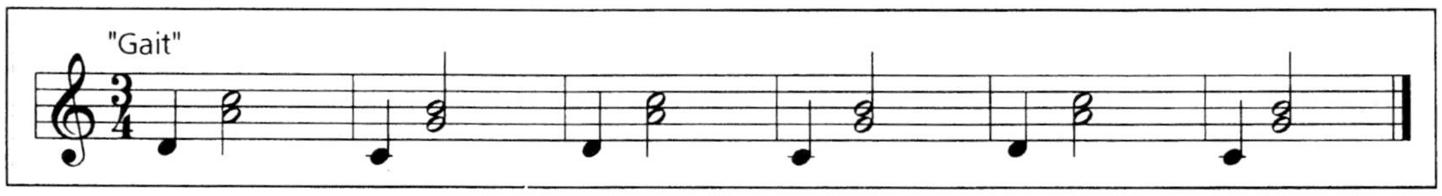

# Minuet in G Major

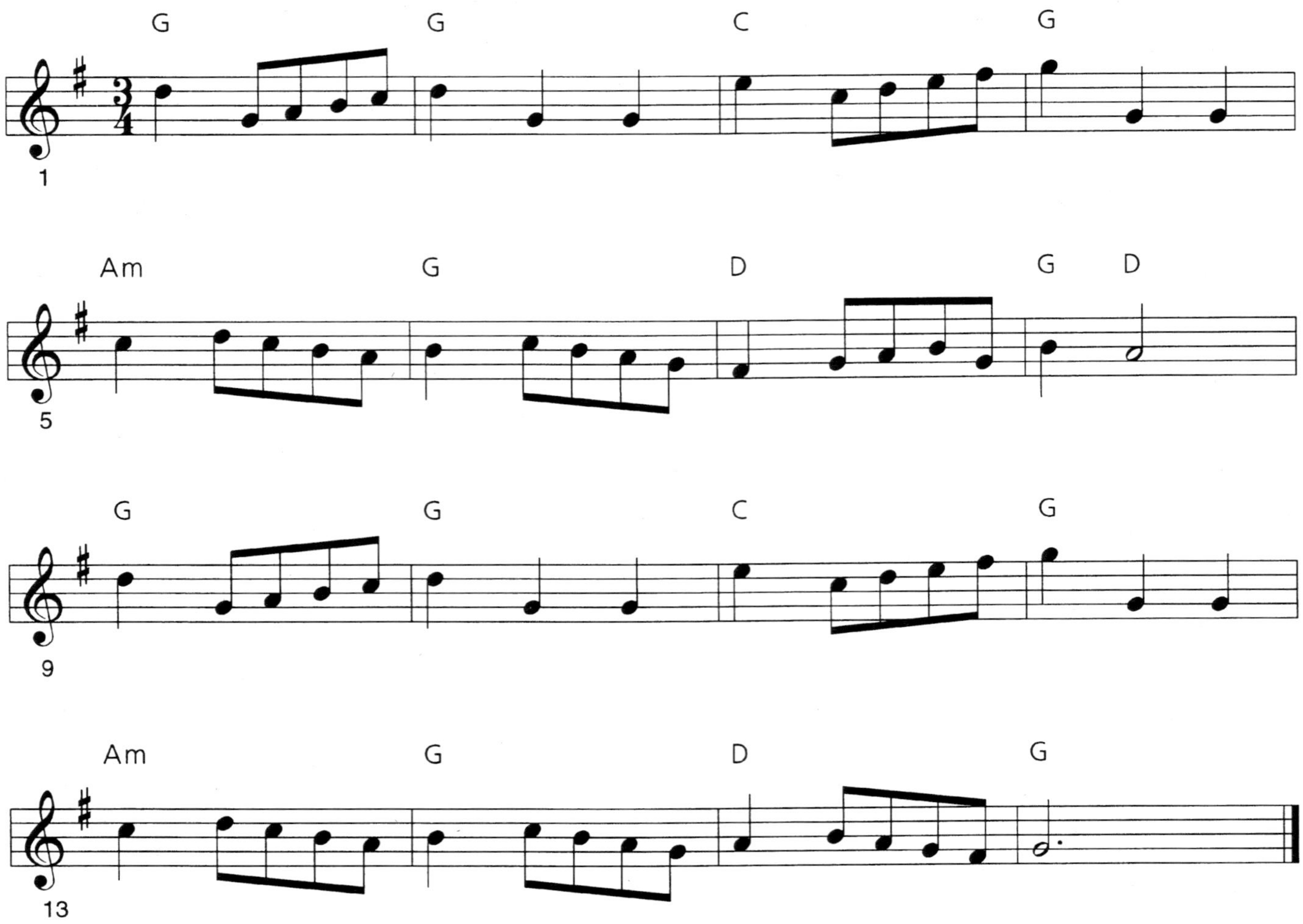


THIS WELL-KNOWN TUNE IS AN EXCELLENT ONE TO PRACTICE FOR "SCALE POSITIONS" (FOUR FINGERS IN A ROW WITH NO STRINGS OPEN IN-BETWEEN)

P.S. DON'T FORGET TO SHARP THE F'S

# Amazing Grace

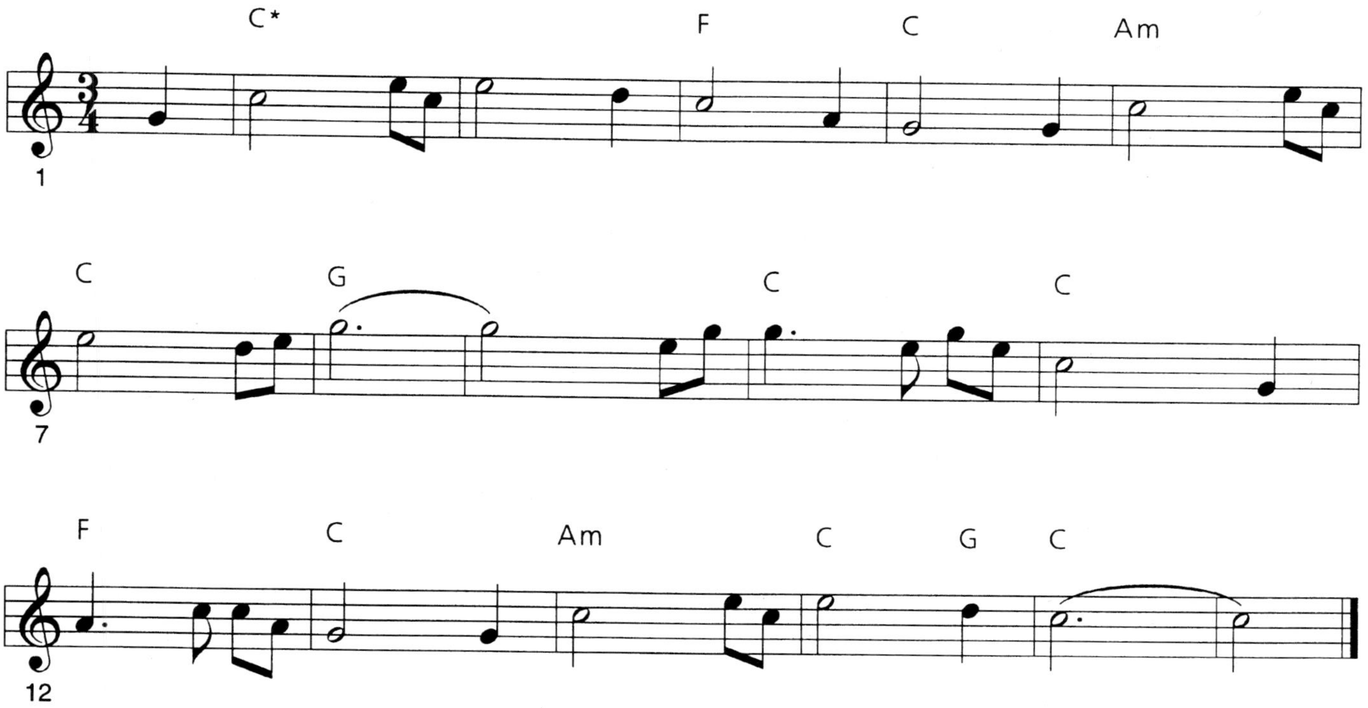


TRY THIS ONE:

A. PLAY WITH A SINGLE-NOTE DRONE.

B. PLAY WITH THE 1 - 5 - 8 PATTERN...

C. FOR A REAL VARIATION WITH SOME SLIGHT DISSONANCE "WALK DOWN" FROM C TO C IN OCTAVES.

* STARTING WITH C ON THE FIRST FULL MEASURE, THEN B... ETC. AND REPEATING THE PROCESS AT THE 10TH MEASURE.

# All Through the Night

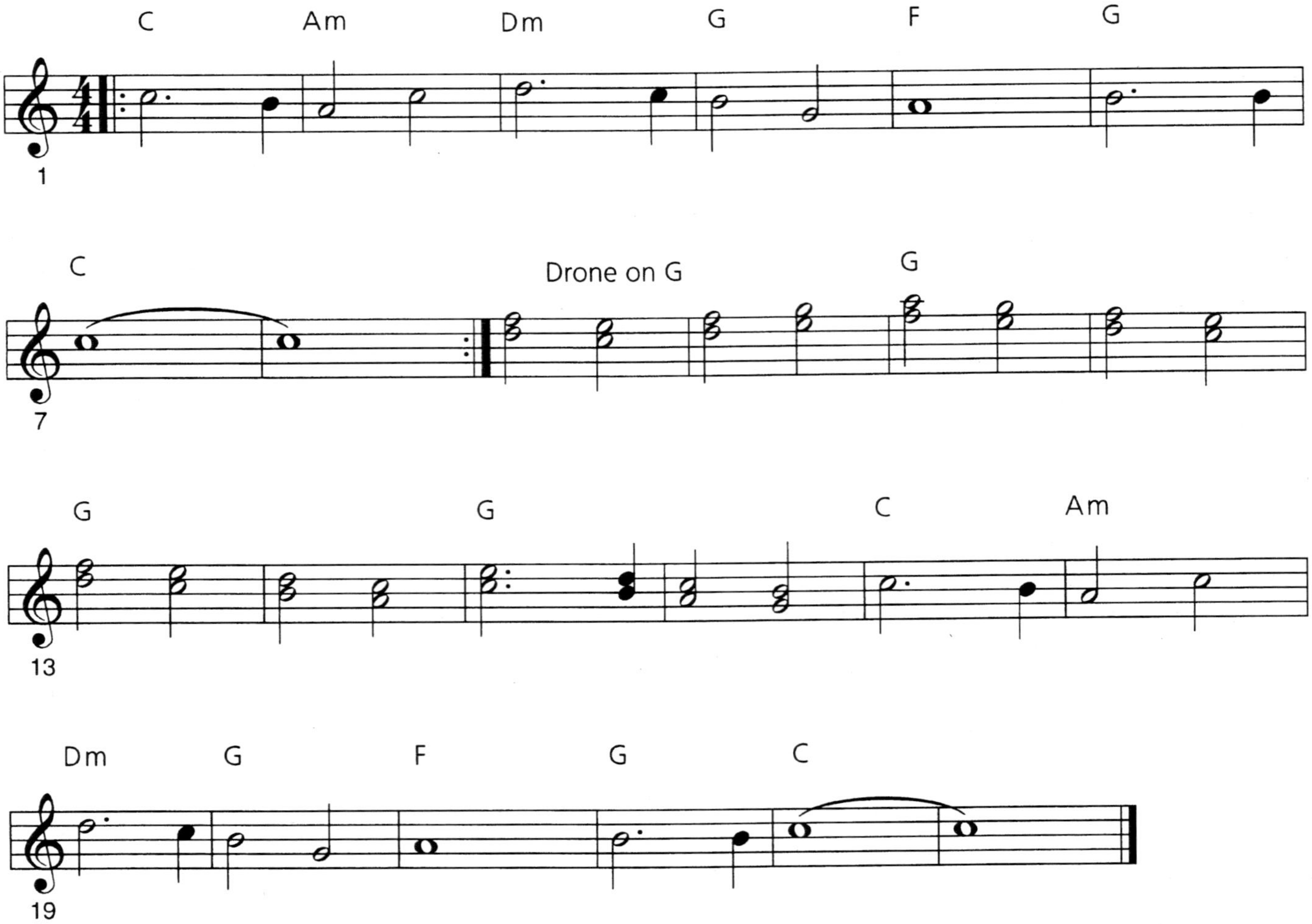


I LIKE THIS SELECTION WITH A SIMPLE DRONE FOLLOWED BY A I - 5 - 8 PATTERN.

YOU TRY IT AND SEE IF YOU AGREE... HAVE FUN!

# The Christ Child's Lullaby

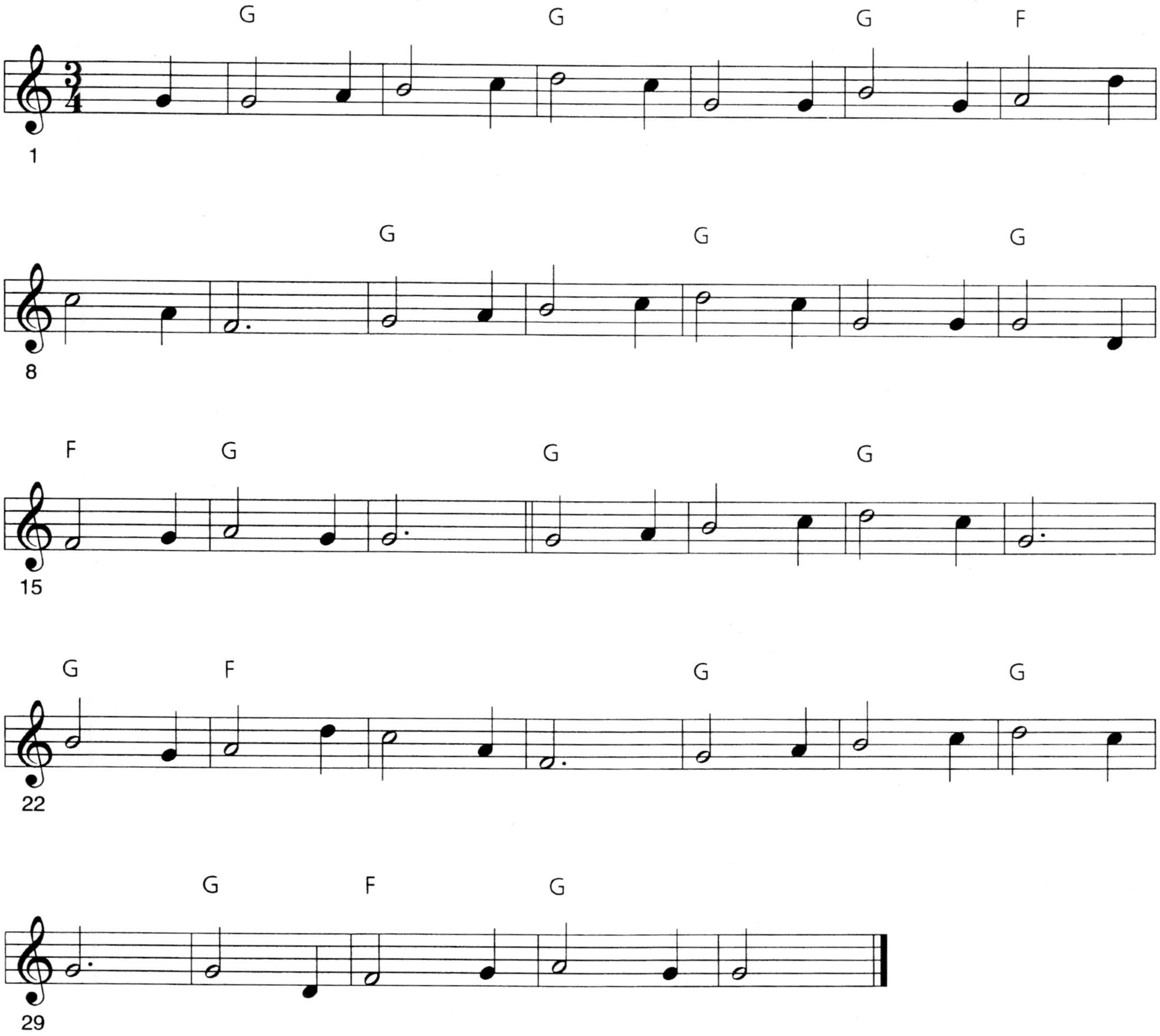


THIS SELECTION IS WONDERFUL WITH ACCOMPANIMENT OF 5THS. THE BOTTOM NOTE OF THE 5TH COMBINATION IS WRITTEN (EXAMPLE: G/D & F/C). THIS IS SIMPLY A TRIAD WITHOUT THE MIDDLE NOTE.

SOUNDS VERY FULL.

# Skye Boat Song

*PLAY G FIRST TIME
*PLAY C SECOND

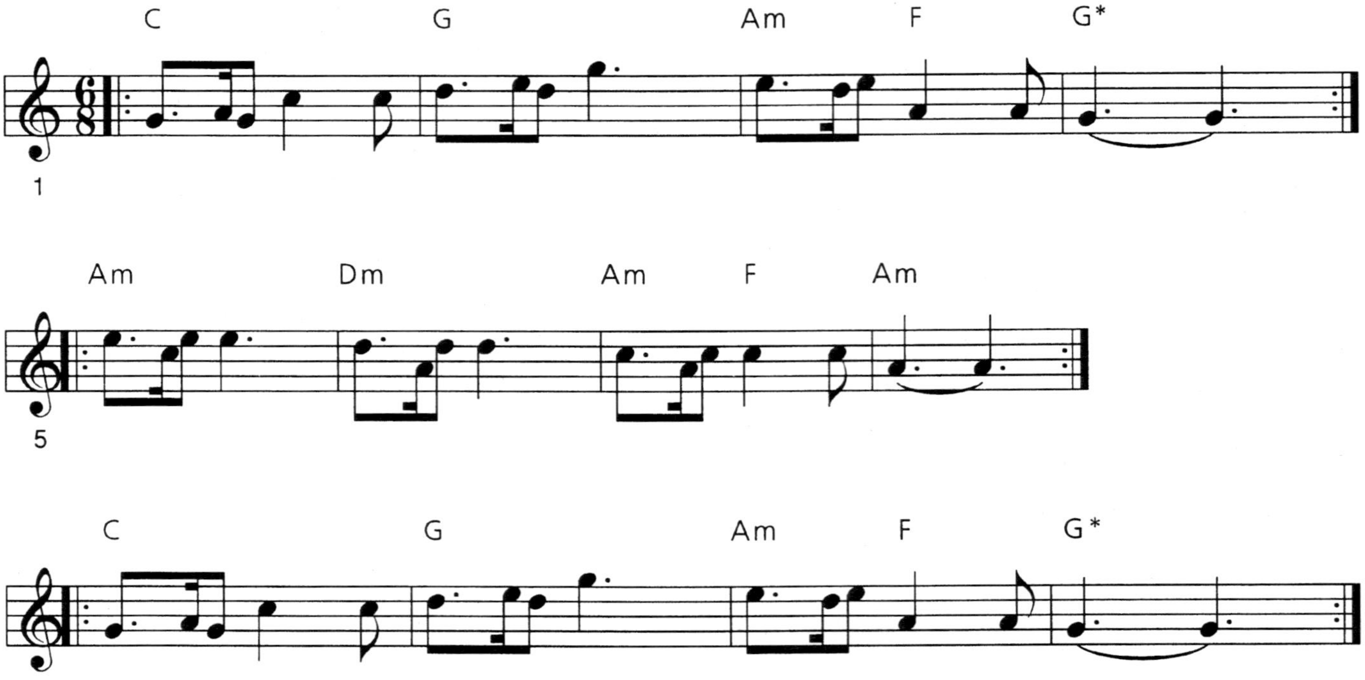


BASED ON THE ACCOMPANIMENT YOU'VE LEARNED SO FAR,
WHAT SOUNDS BEST TO YOU?

BROKEN PATTERNS LIKE ROVING THUMBS?

1 - 5 - 8?

OPEN 5THS?

ROLLS?

SPLIT OCTAVES?

DRONES?

# Greensleeves

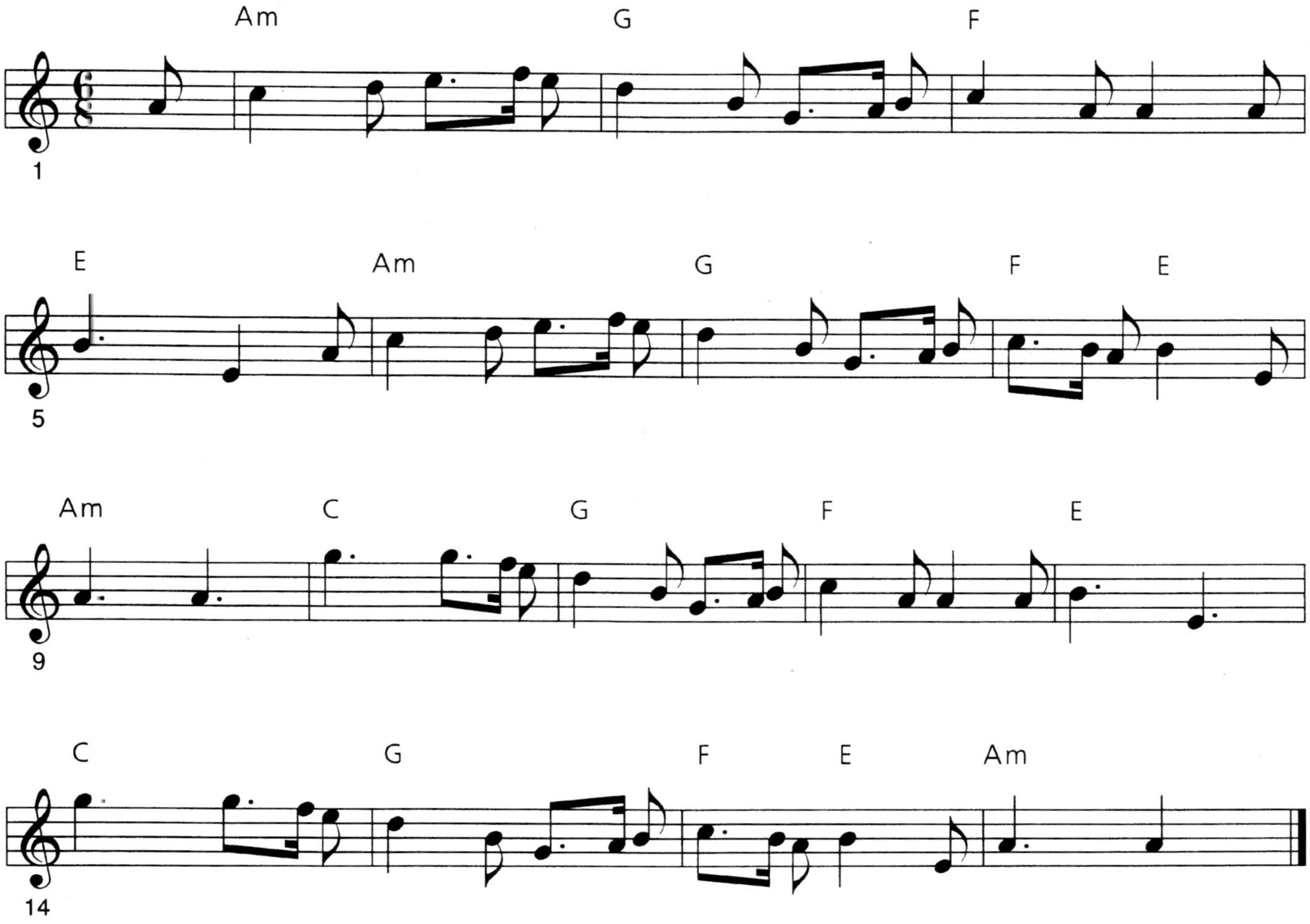


THIS TUNE CAN BE EASILY BUILT FROM A SIMPLE ACCOMPANIMENT LIKE A:

DRONE

TO A TRIAD, ON TO A 1 - 5 - 8 AND

FINALLY A 1 - 5 - 8 - 5 - 10

BEFORE ENDING ON A DRONE.

A VERY DRAMATIC EFFECT!

# Brian Boru's March

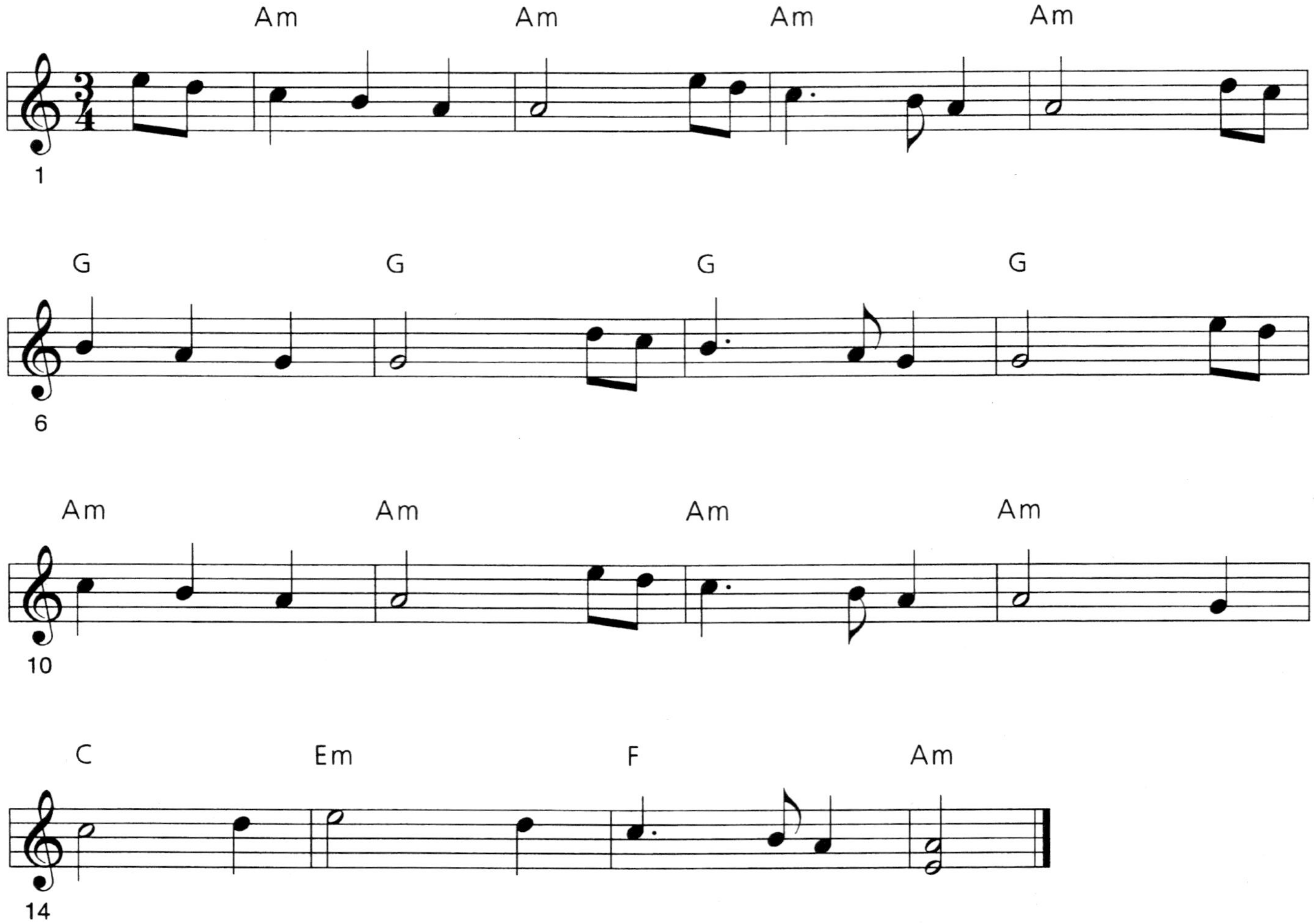


THIS TUNE CAN ADAPT EASILY TO:

A. DRONE

B. TRIAD

C. 1 - 5 - 8

D. 5THS

E. OCTAVES

F. SPLIT OCTAVES

PLAY WITH THIS MELODY... AND CREATE YOUR OWN "IRISH" EFFECT.

# Flow Gently, Sweet Afton

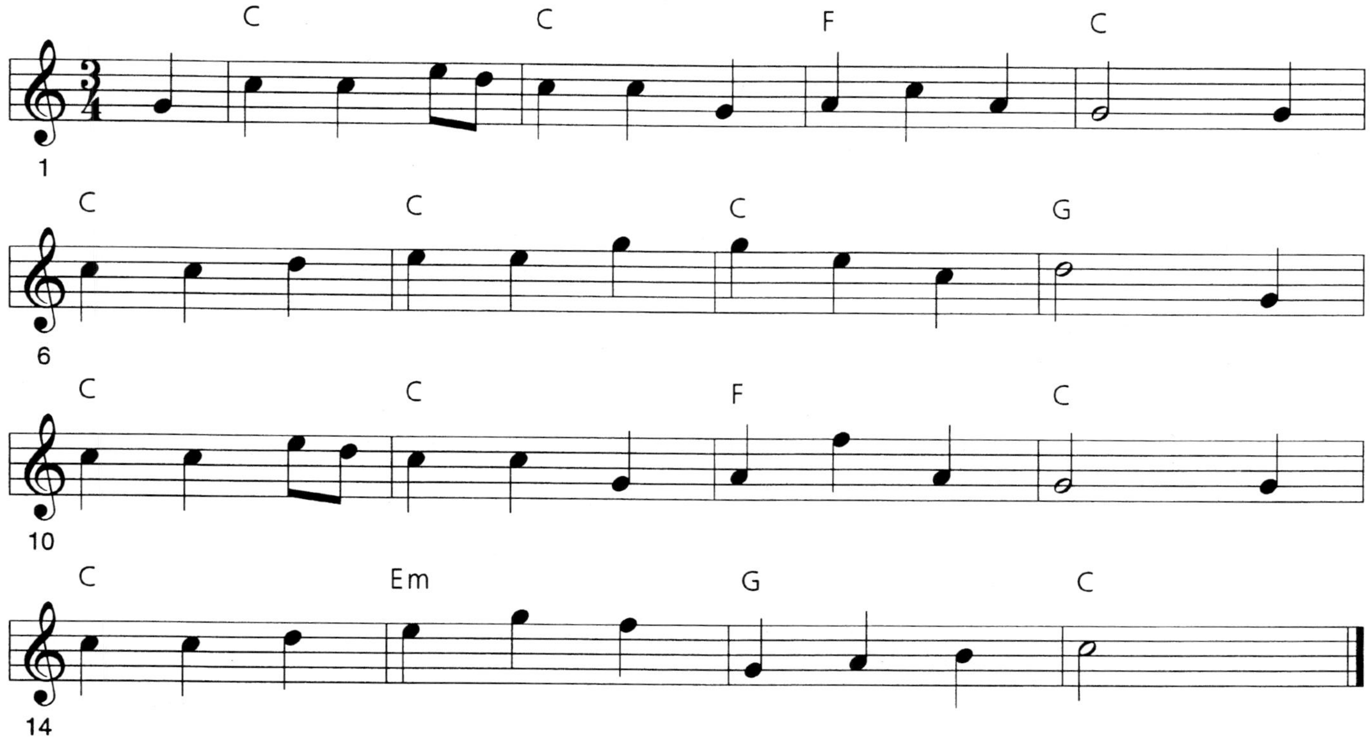


A 1 - 5 - 8 ACCOMPANIMENT FITS IN QUICKLY WITH THIS TUNE,
BUT WHAT ELSE DO YOU HEAR THAT COULD BE USED?

# The Grenadier and the Lady

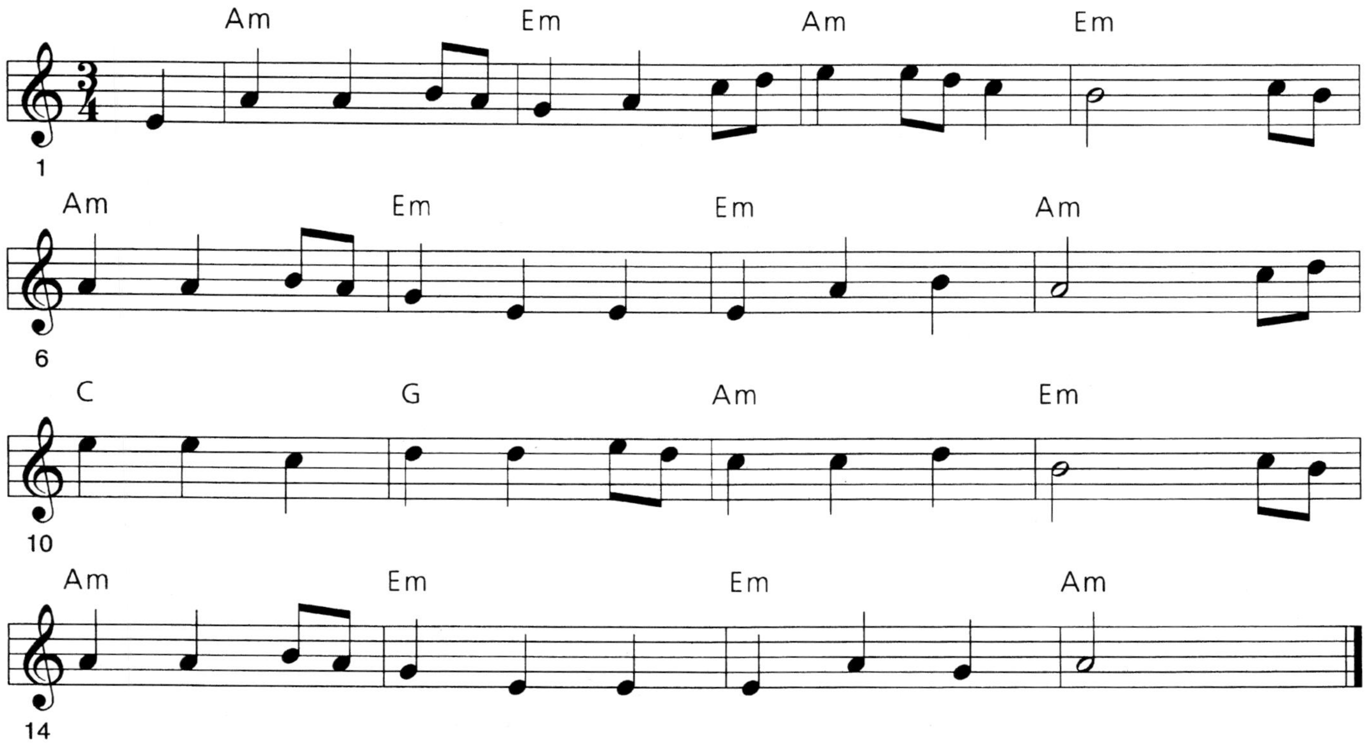


A DRONE THE FIRST TIME THROUGH FOLLOWED BY THE 1 - 5 - 8
GIVES A CELTIC FLAVOR TO THIS MELODY.

# On Top of Old Smoky

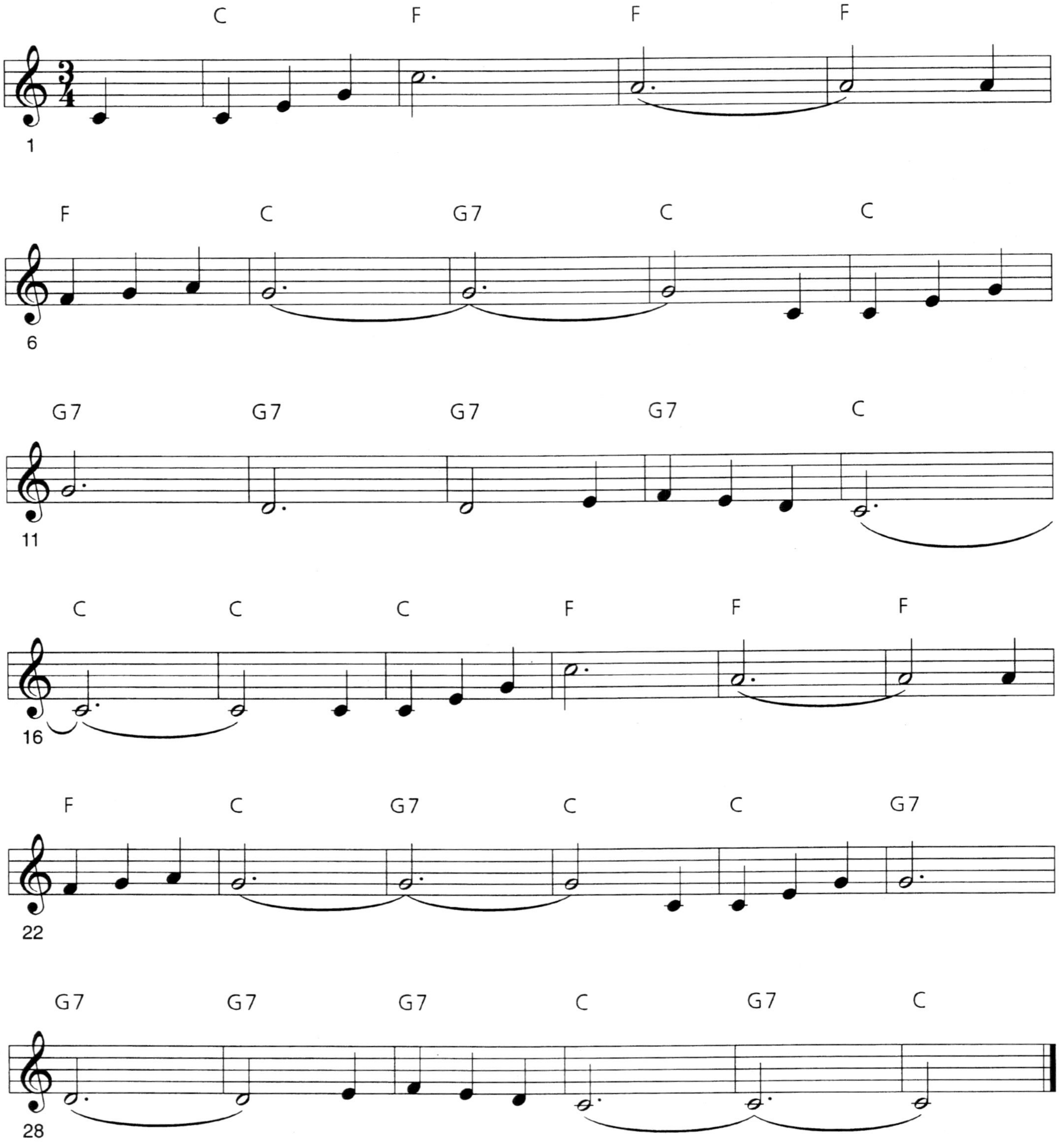

# The Star of the County Down

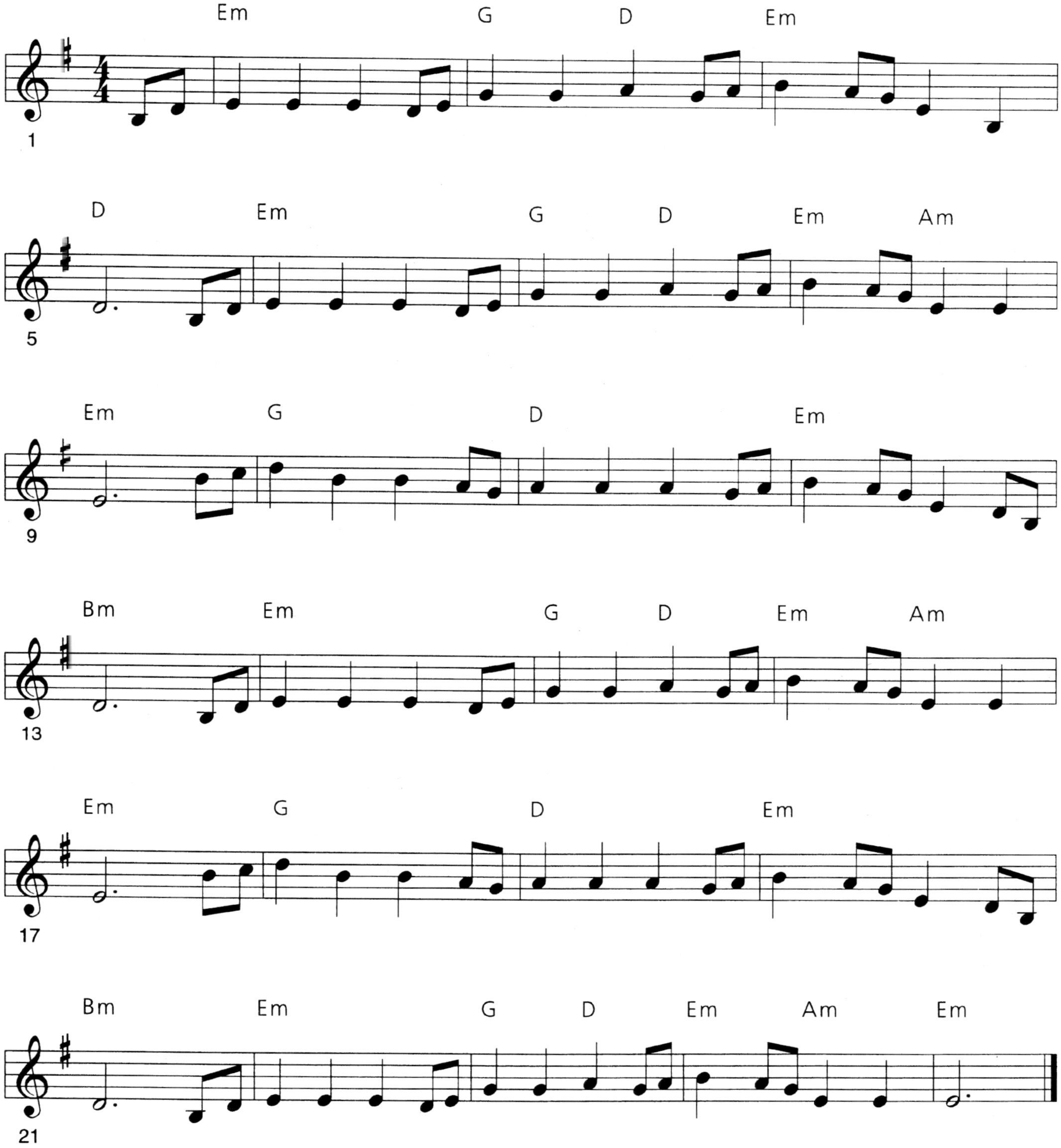

# The Sally Gardens

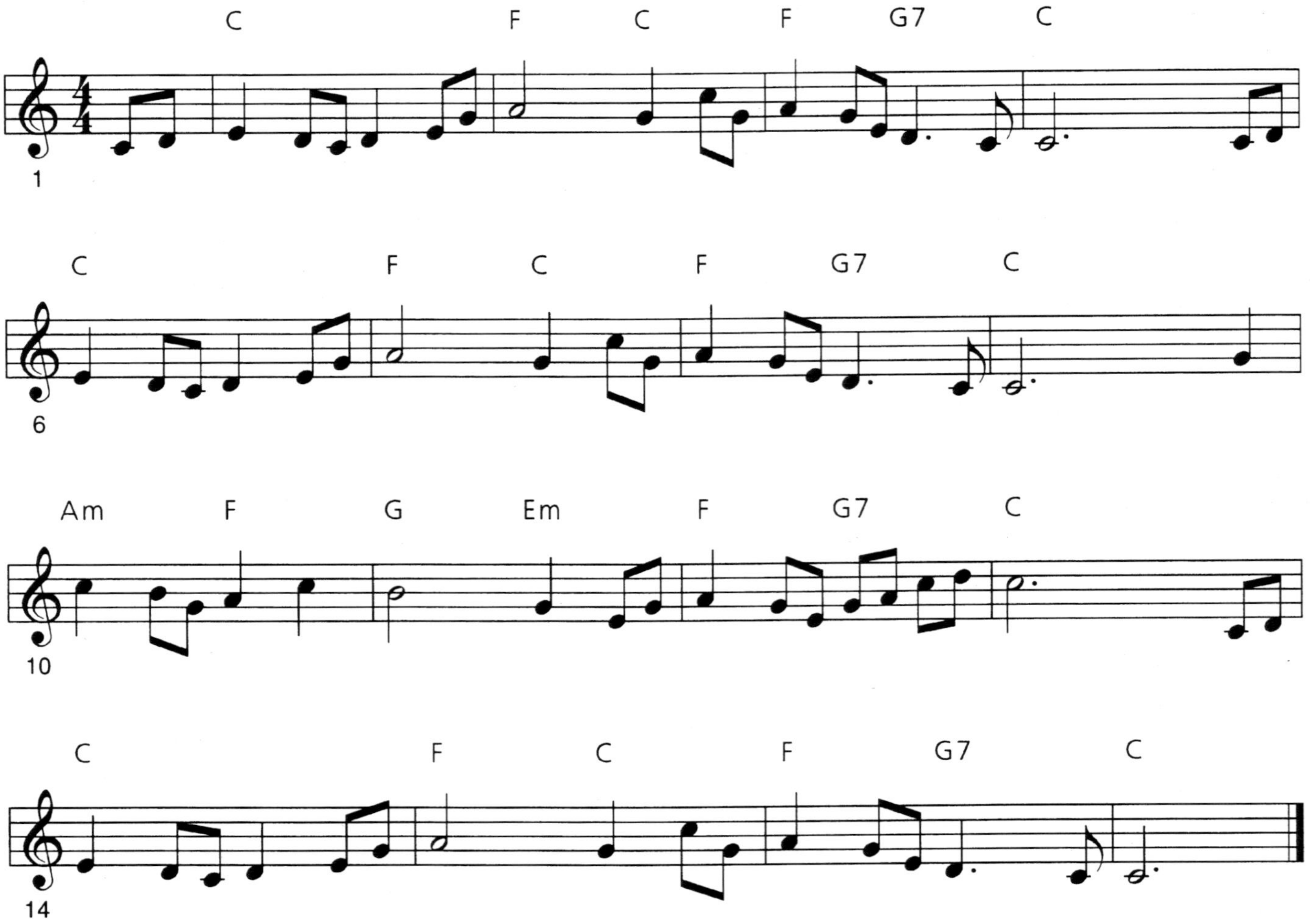


FIFTHS ON THE 1 - 5 - 8 PATTERN

WORK WELL WITH THIS MELODY.

# Simple Gifts

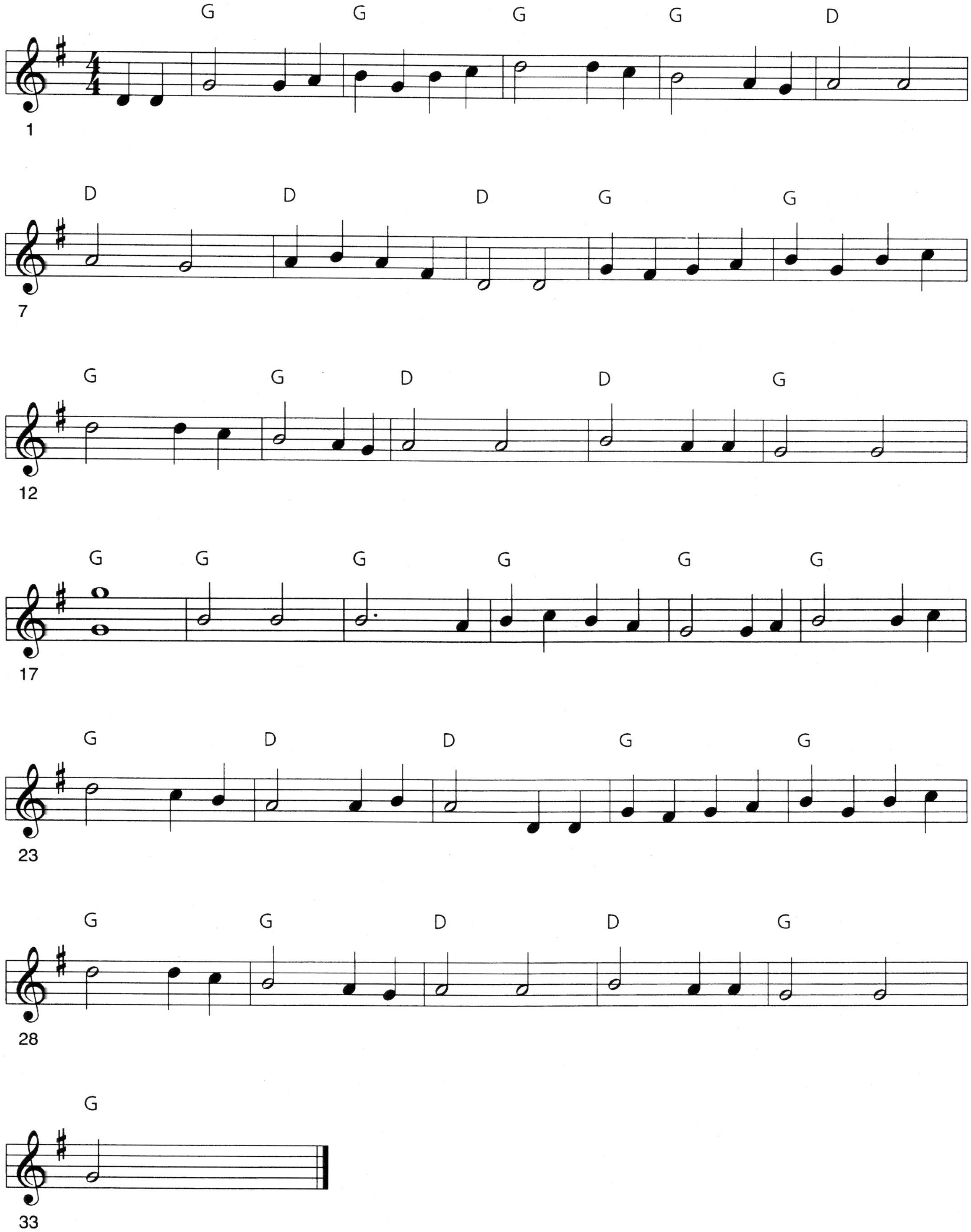

# When the Saints Go Marching In

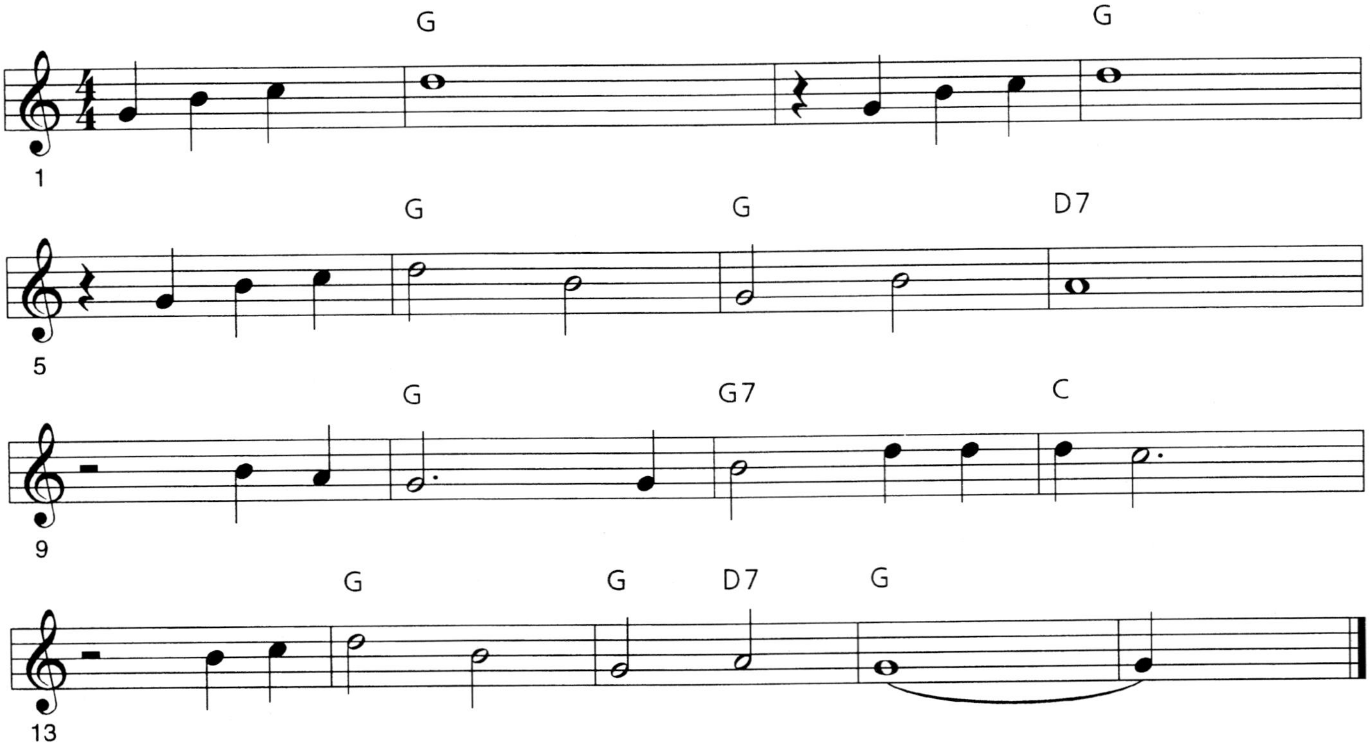


# Jingle Bells

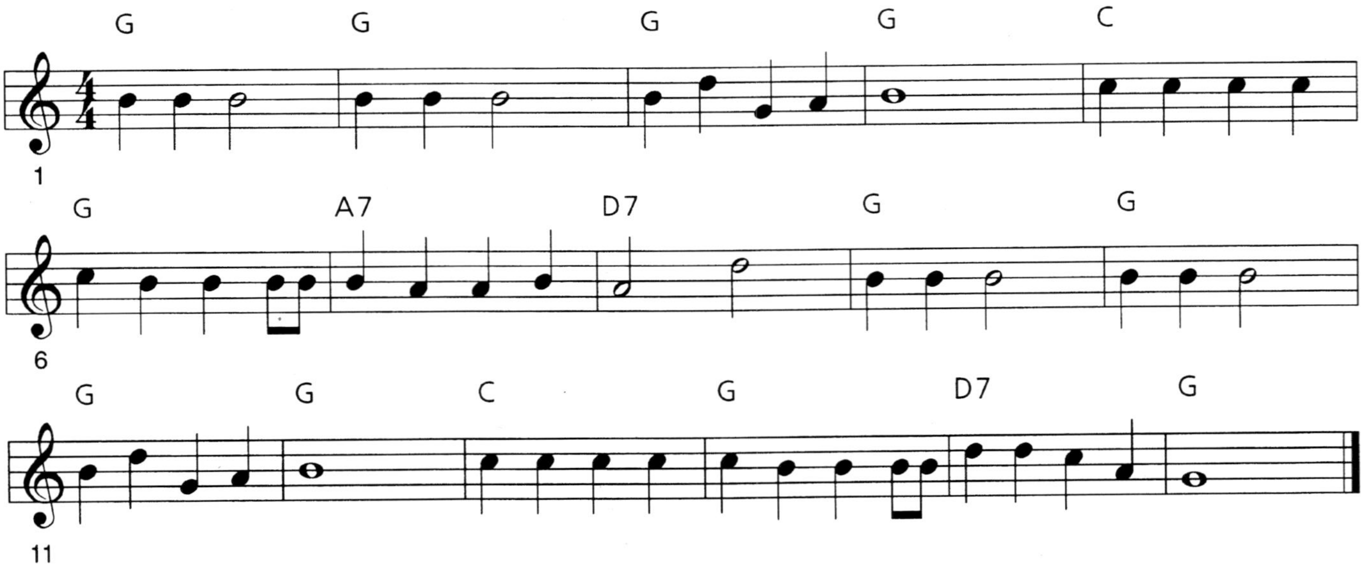


FOR A REAL CHALLENGE, TRY THIS ONE USING HARMONICS

(A METHOD OF PLAYING A STRING SO THAT IT SOUNDS
AN OCTAVE HIGHER THAN ITS NORMAL PITCH).

# The Ash Grove

Wales

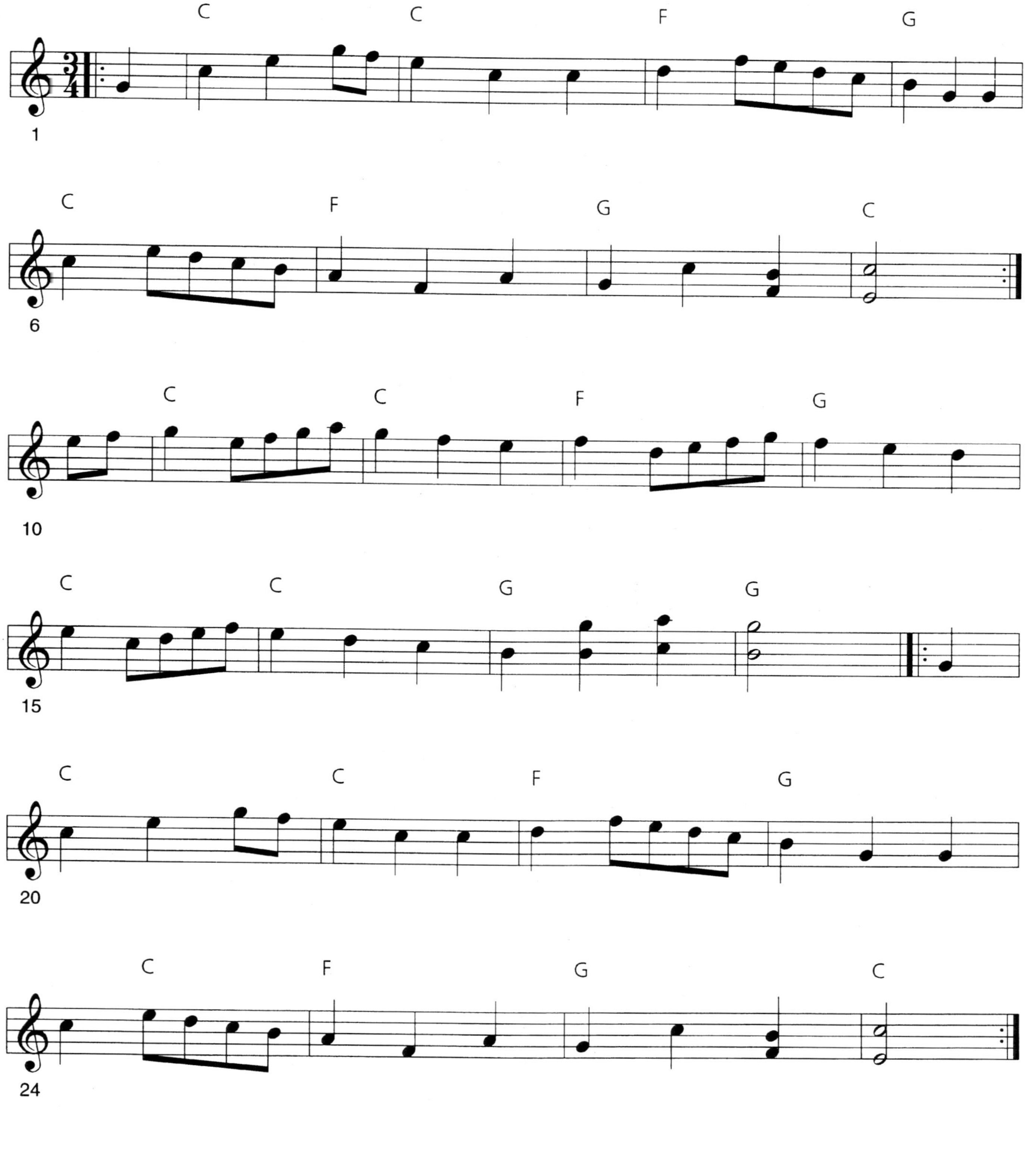

# Jacob's Ladder

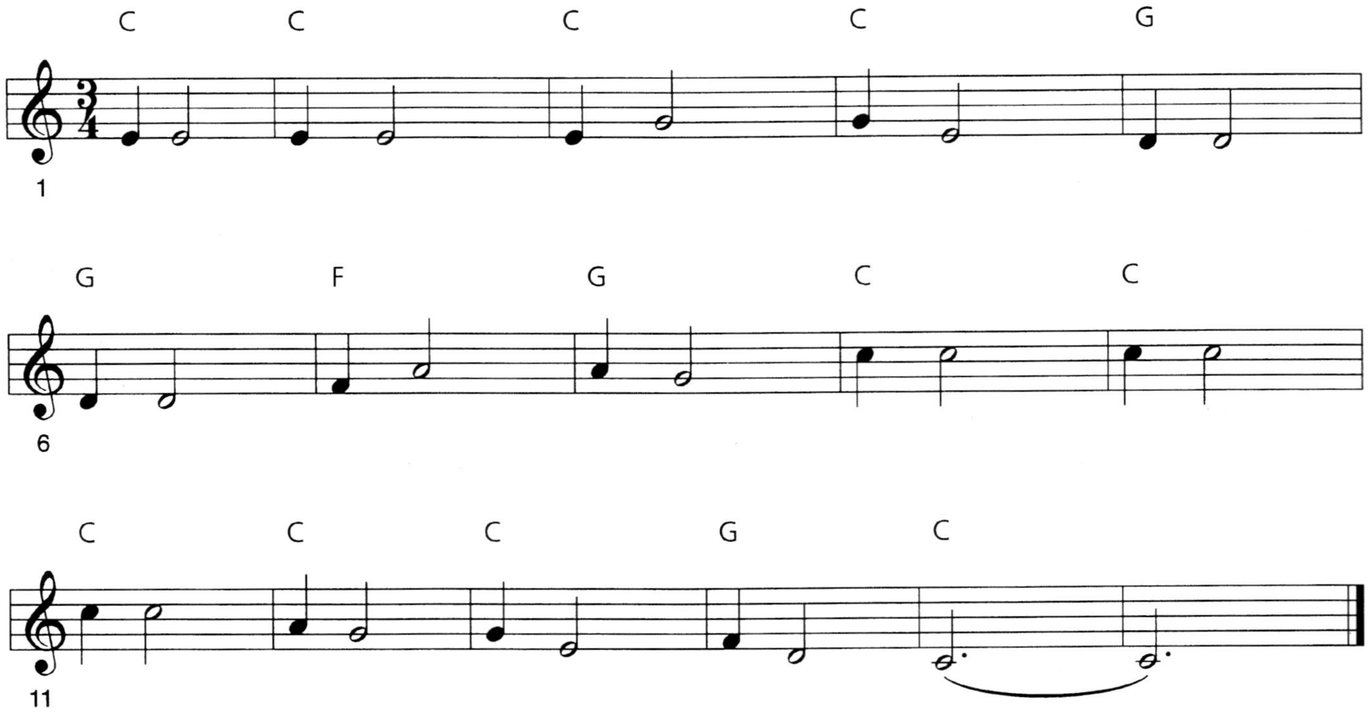


THIS IS A GOOD SONG TO START

SIMPLY WITH A DRONE AND

THEN CONTINUE TO BUILD WITH SEVERAL OTHER LEFT-HAND

TECHNIQUES... ENDING WITH THE GARRETT.

# White Coral Bells

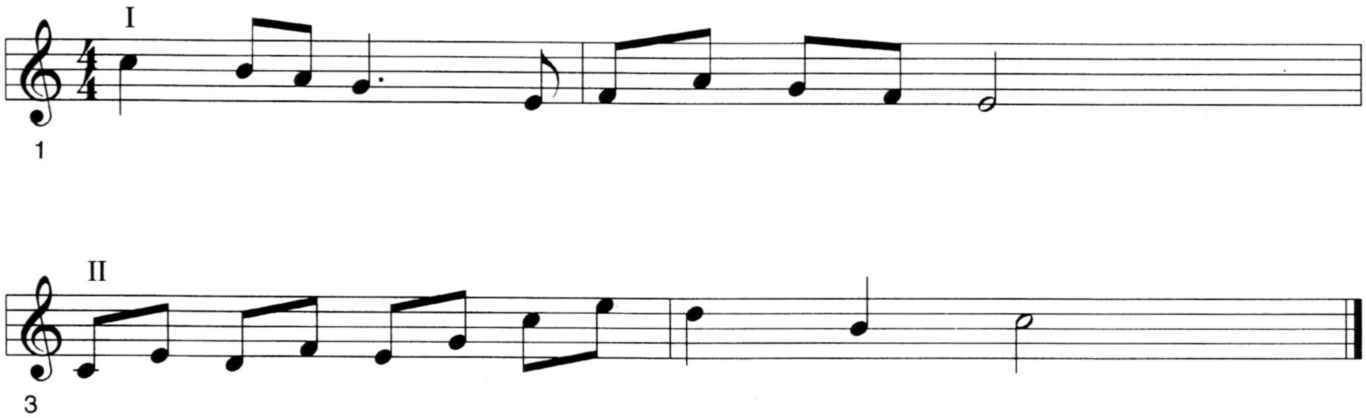


# Brother John

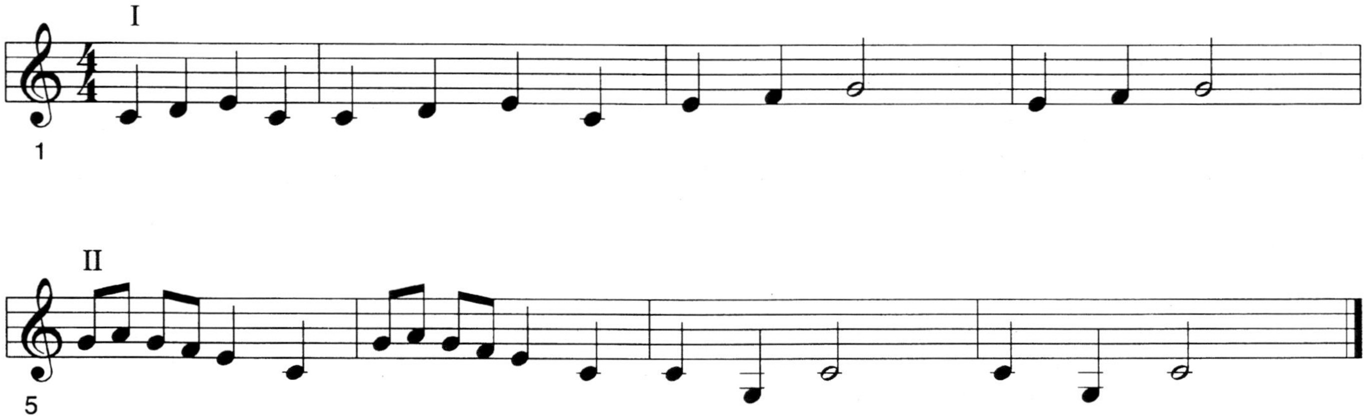


# Music Alone Shall Live

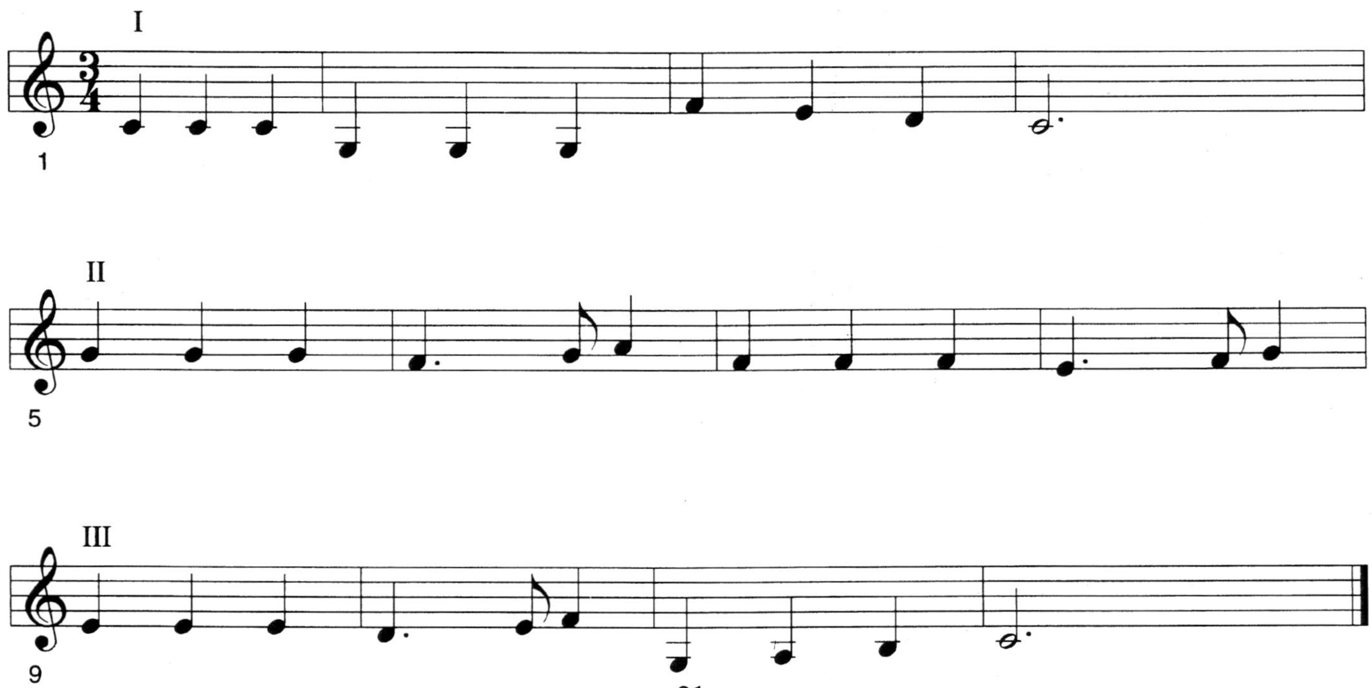

# Dona Nobis Pacem

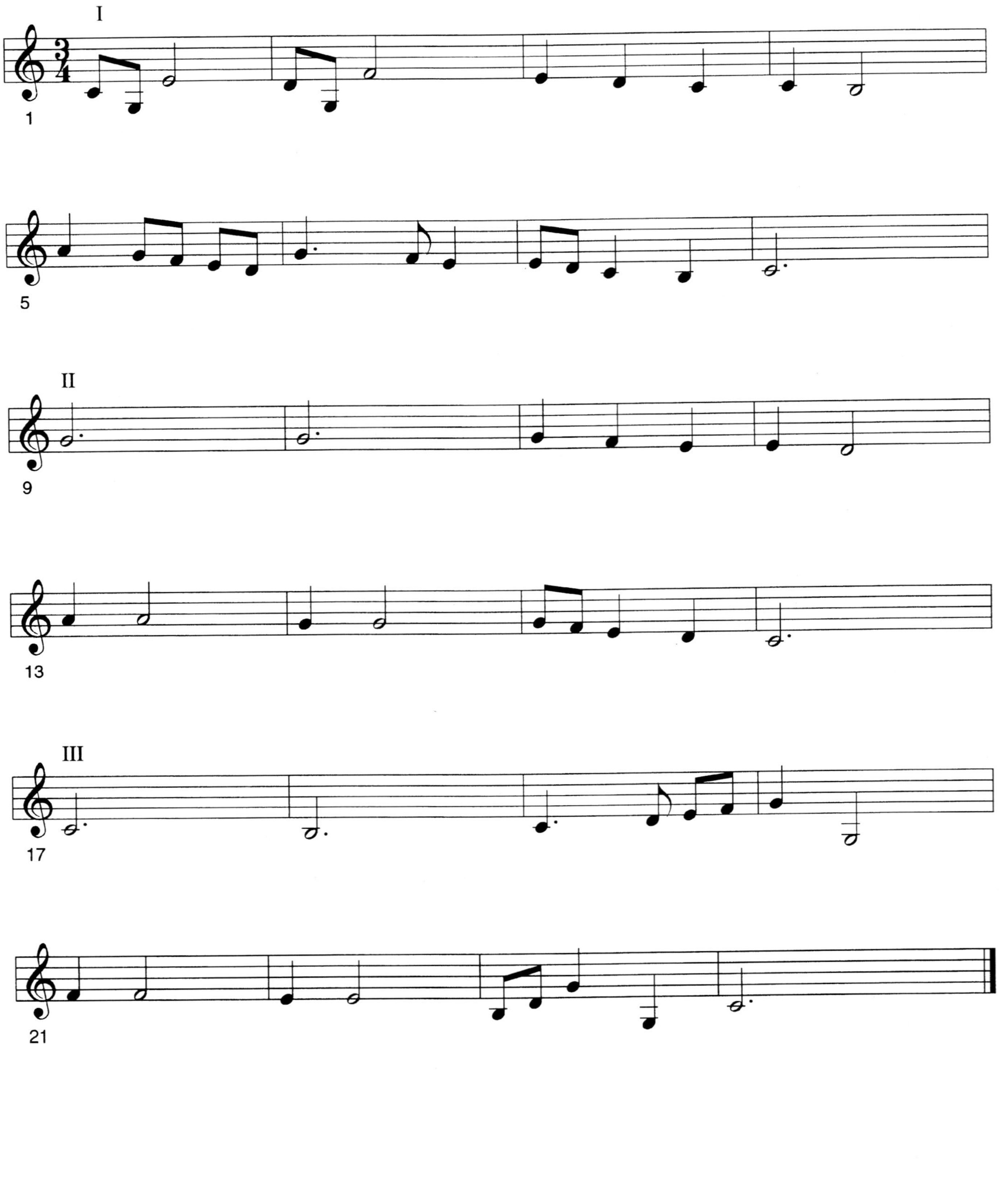

# Shalom Chaverim

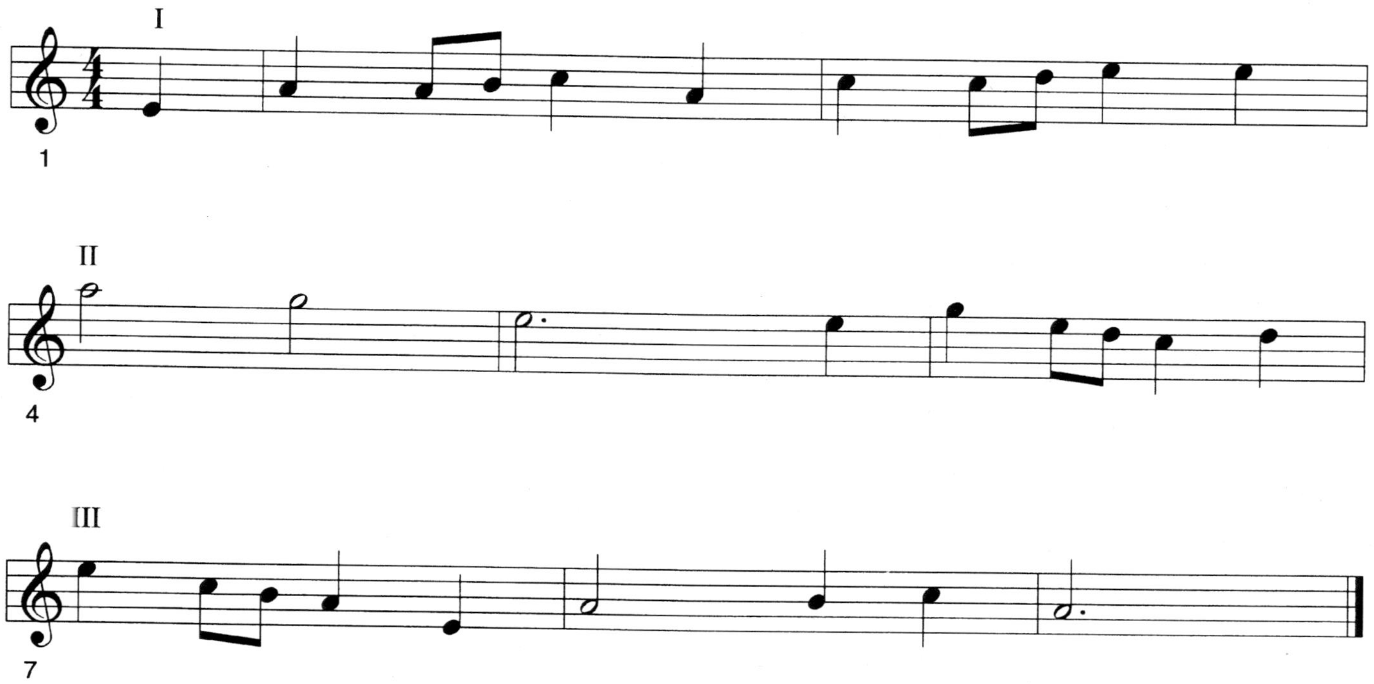


# Tanz

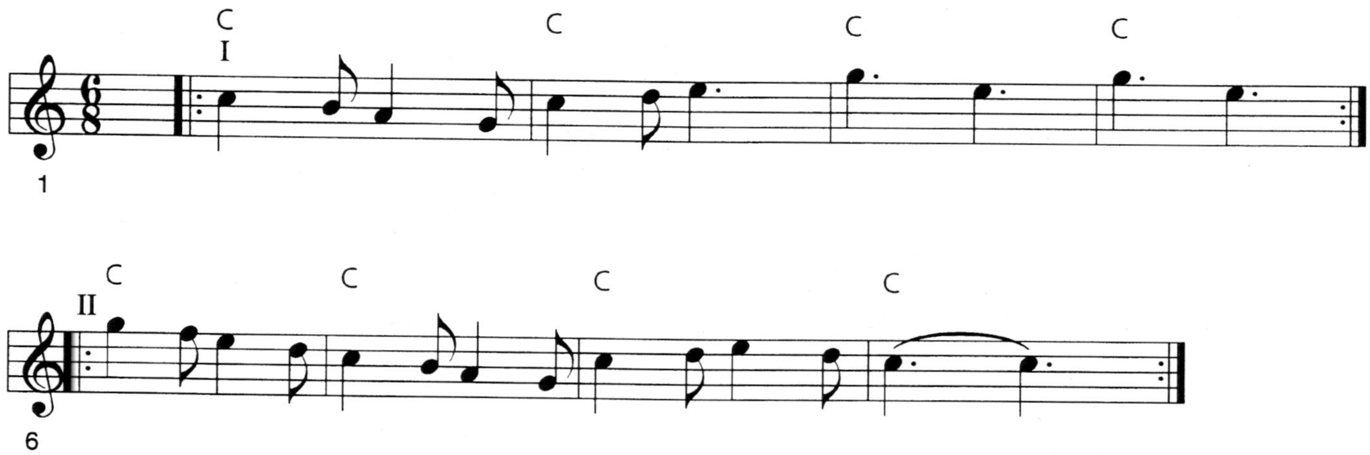

# William's Lullaby

Sue Raimond

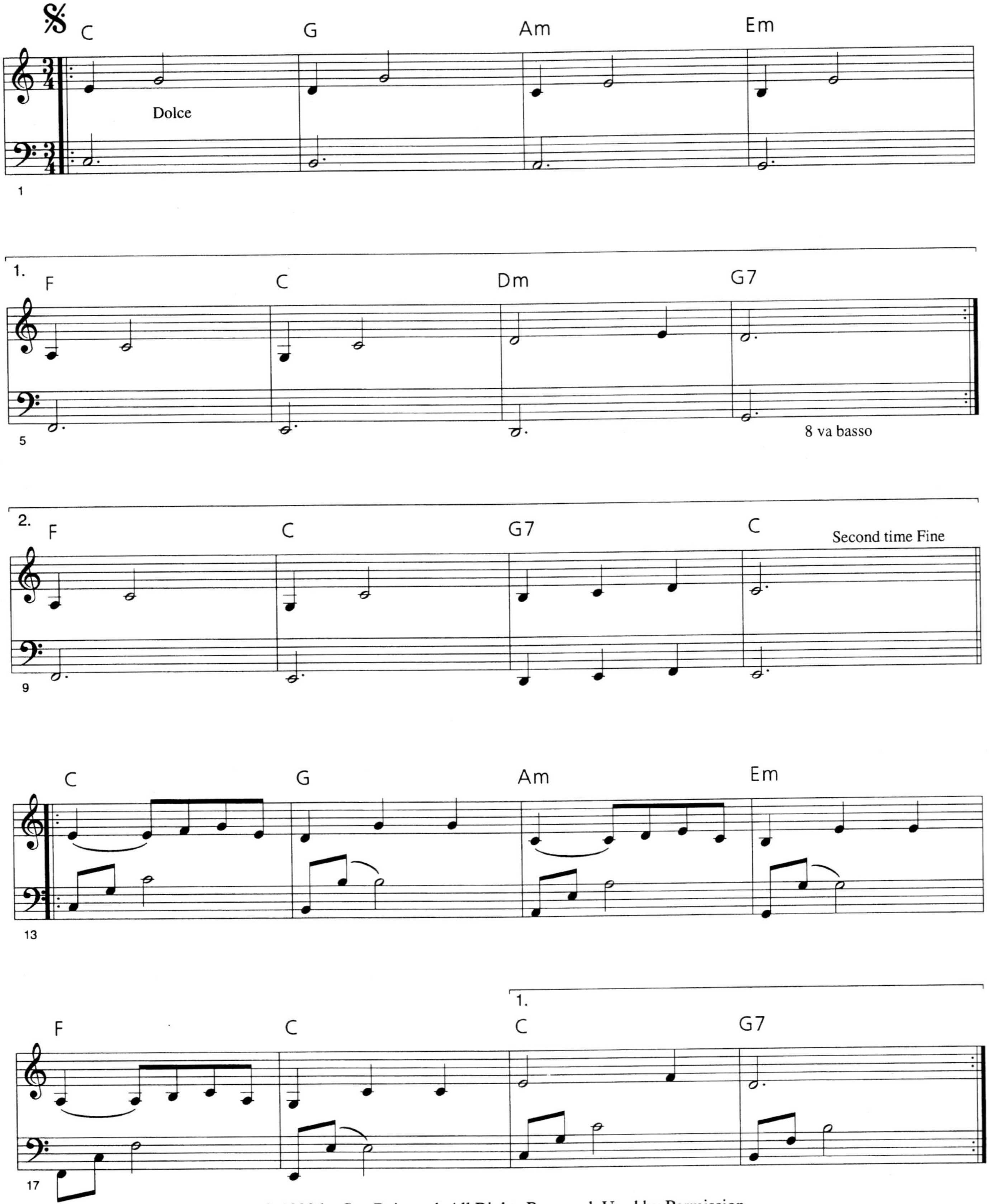

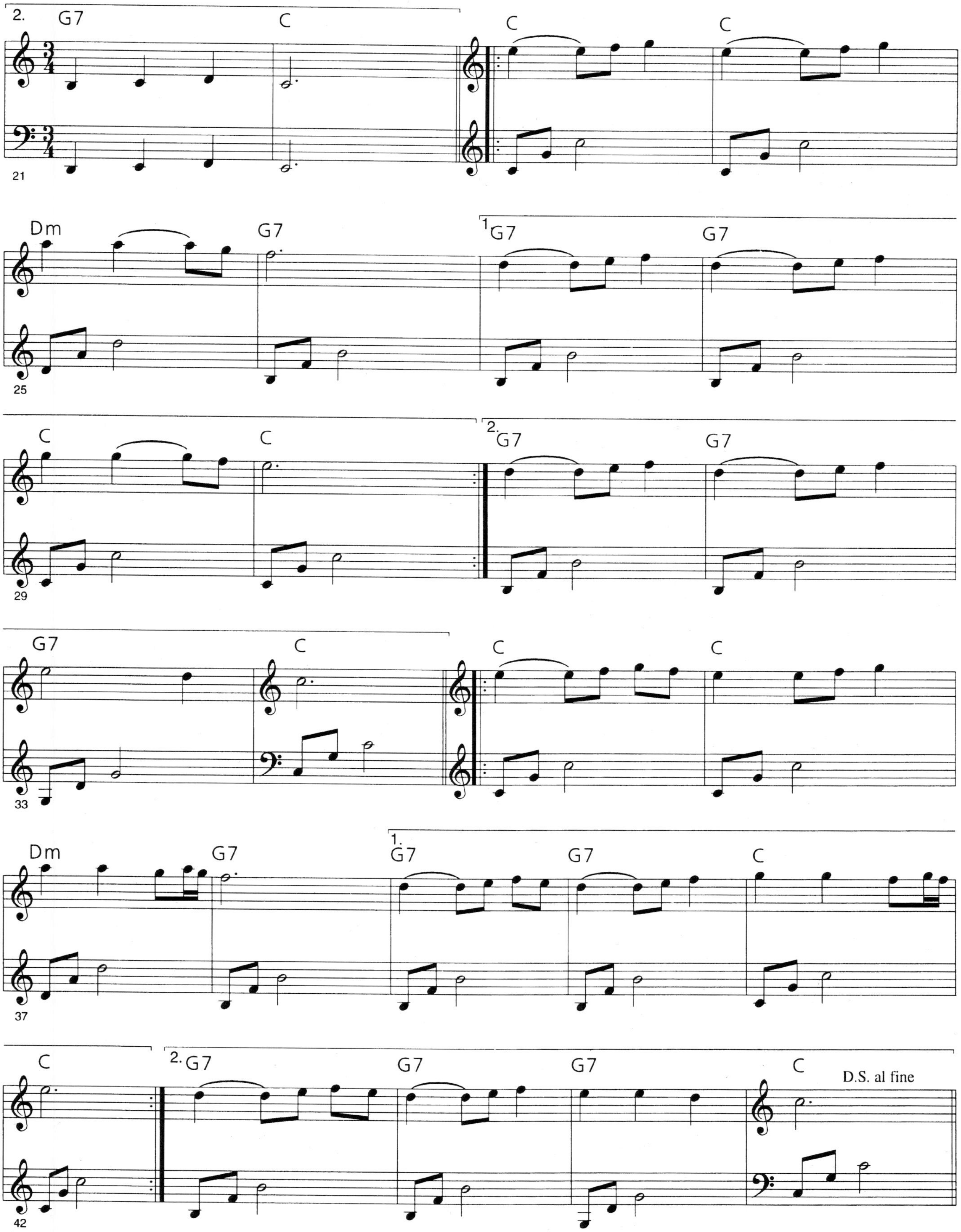

2.
G7
C
C
C
21
Dm
G7
1
G7
G7
25
C
C
2.
G7
G7
29
G7
C
C
C
33
Dm
G7
1.
G7
G7
C
37
C
2.
G7
G7
G7
C
D.S. al fine
42

# Gentry's Gait

Sue Raimond

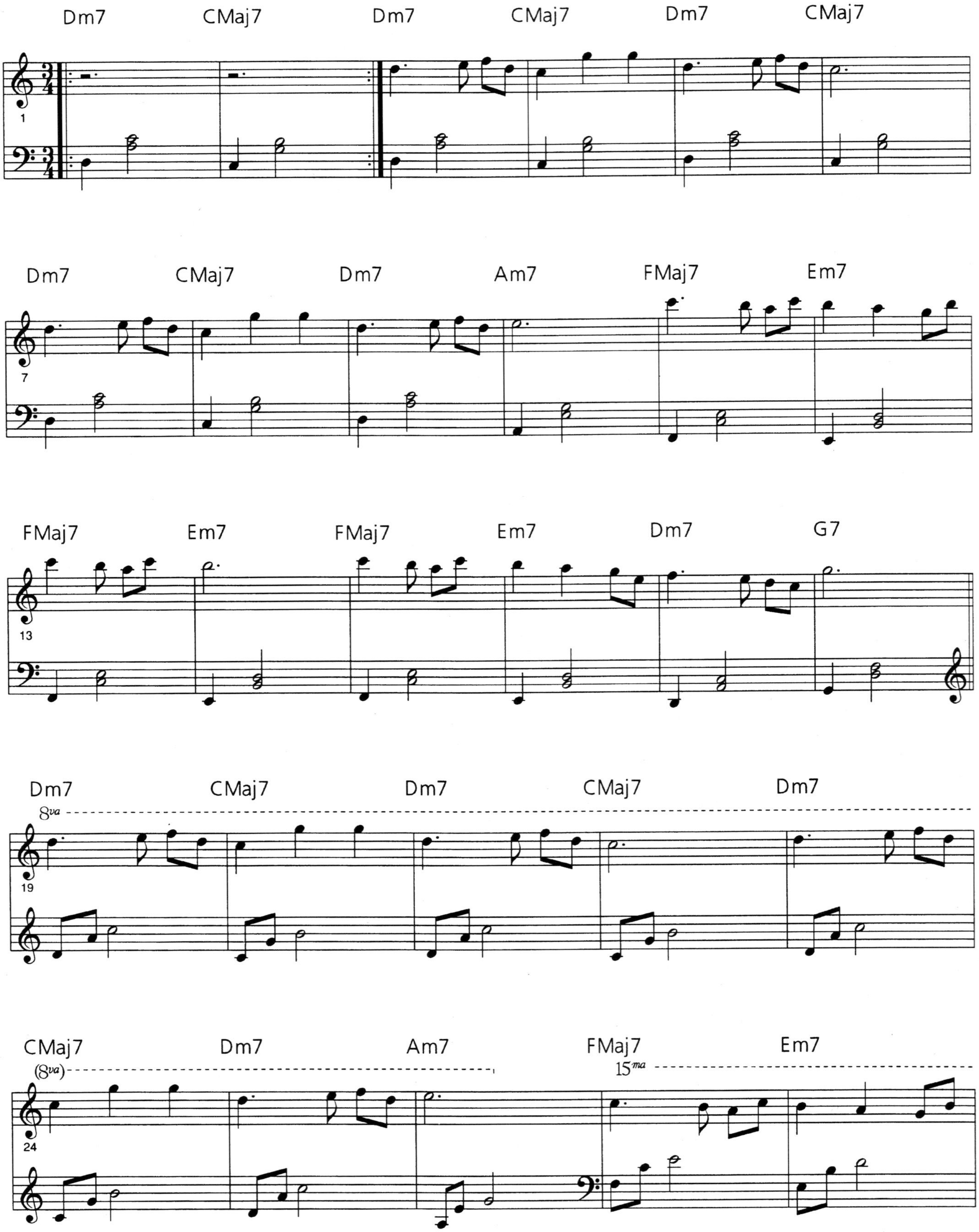

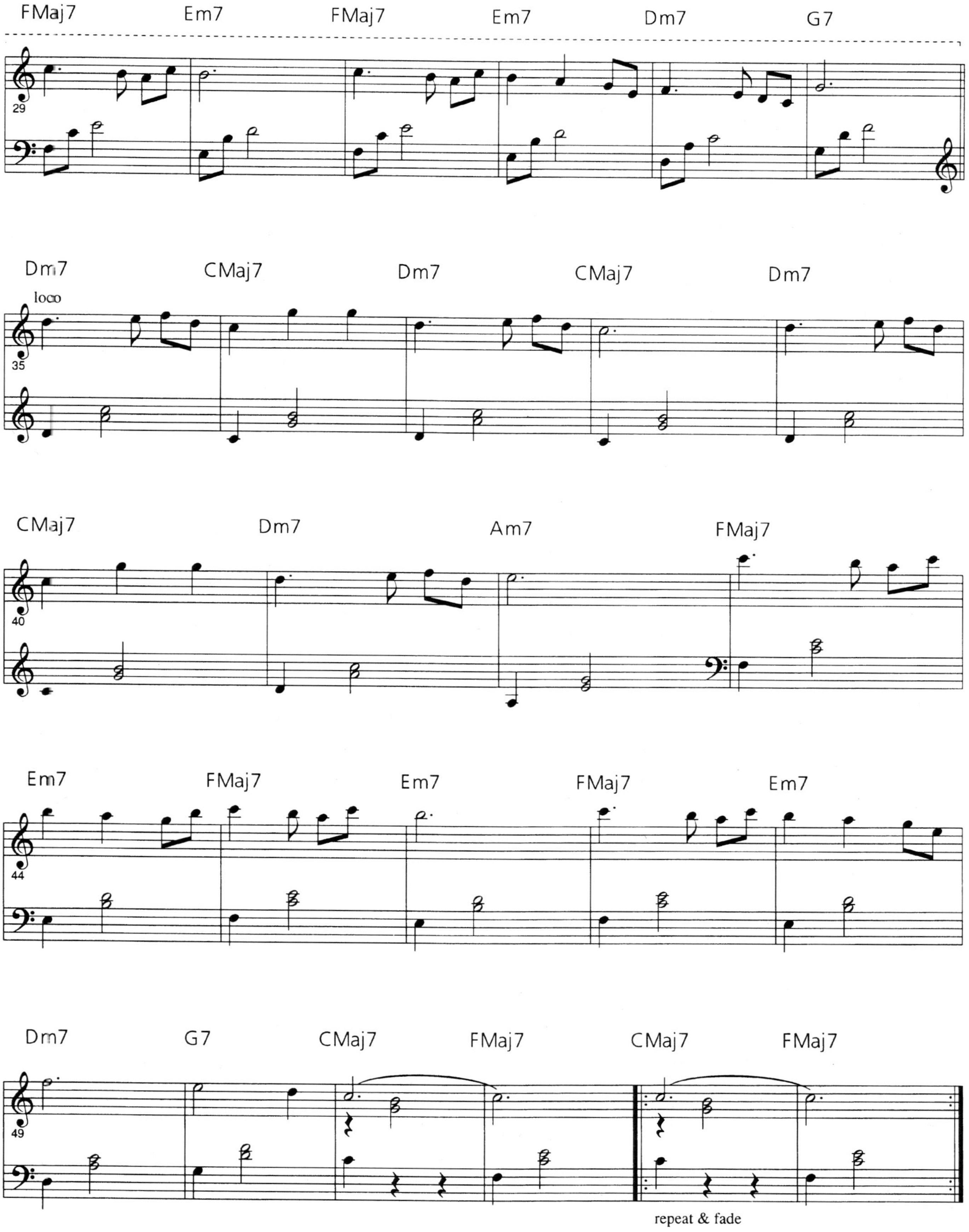
FMaj7 Em7 FMaj7 Em7 Dm7 G7
29
Dm7 CMaj7 Dm7 CMaj7 Dm7
loco
35
CMaj7 Dm7 Am7 FMaj7
40
Em7 FMaj7 Em7 FMaj7 Em7
44
Dm7 G7 CMaj7 FMaj7 CMaj7 FMaj7
49
repeat & fade

# Matilija

Sue Raimond

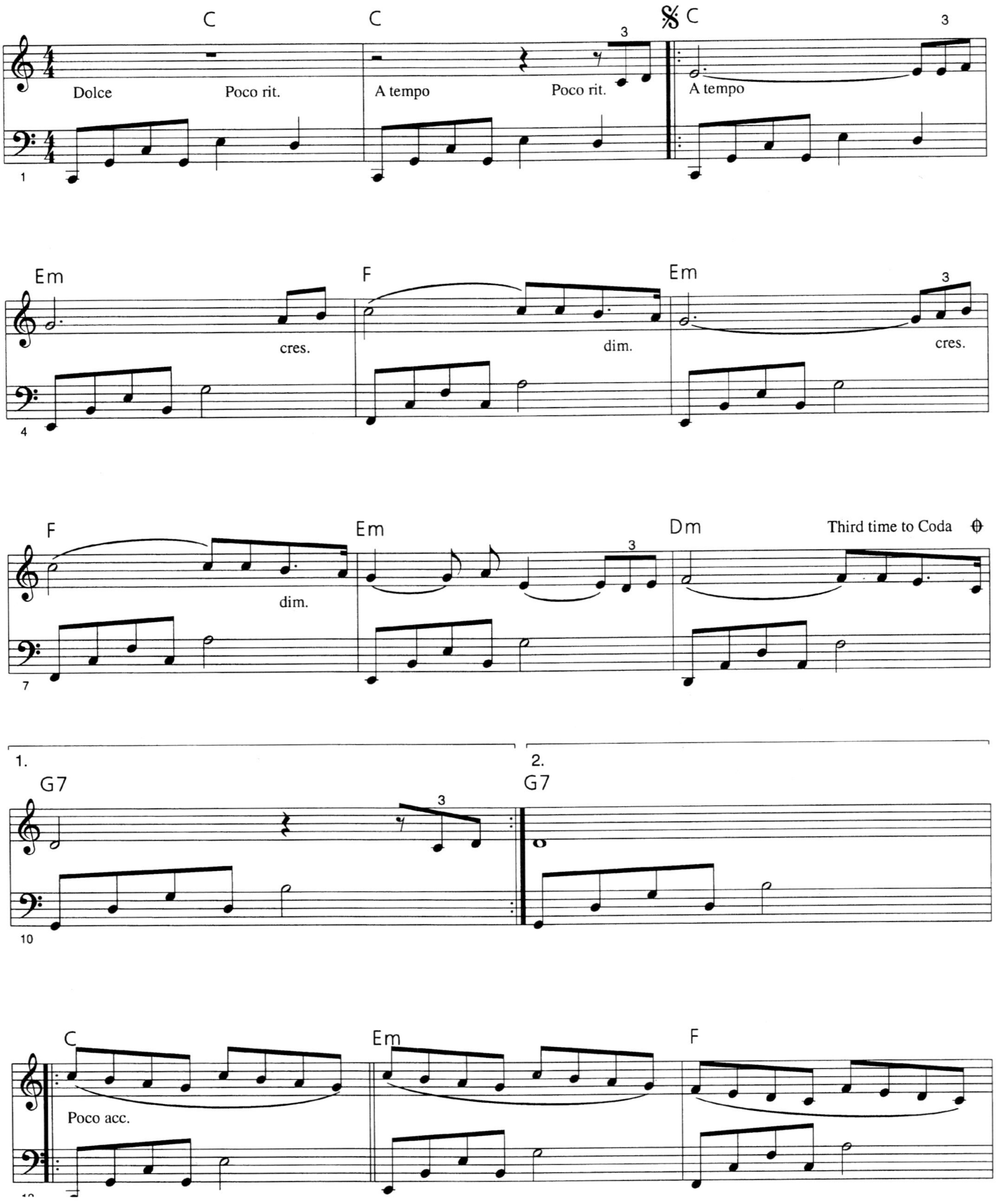

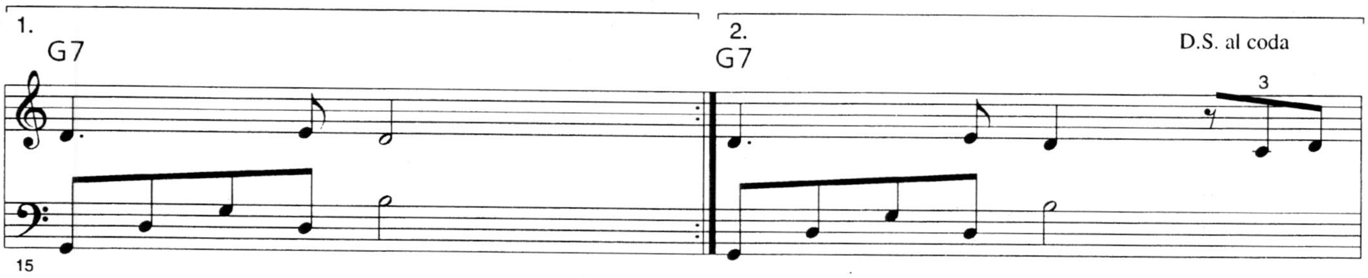
1.
G7
2.
G7
D.S. al coda
3
15

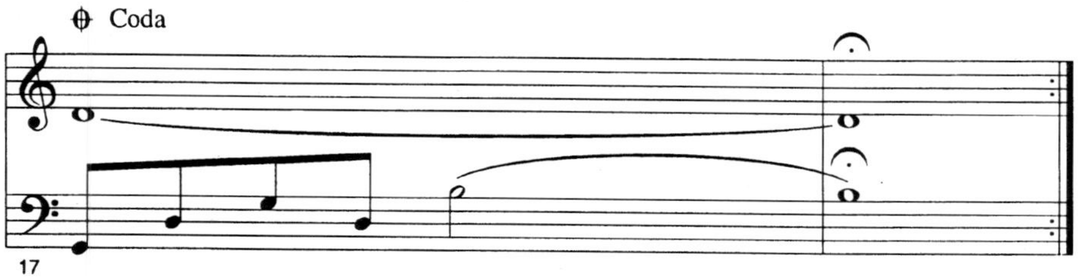
Coda
17

# Aliso

Sue Raimond

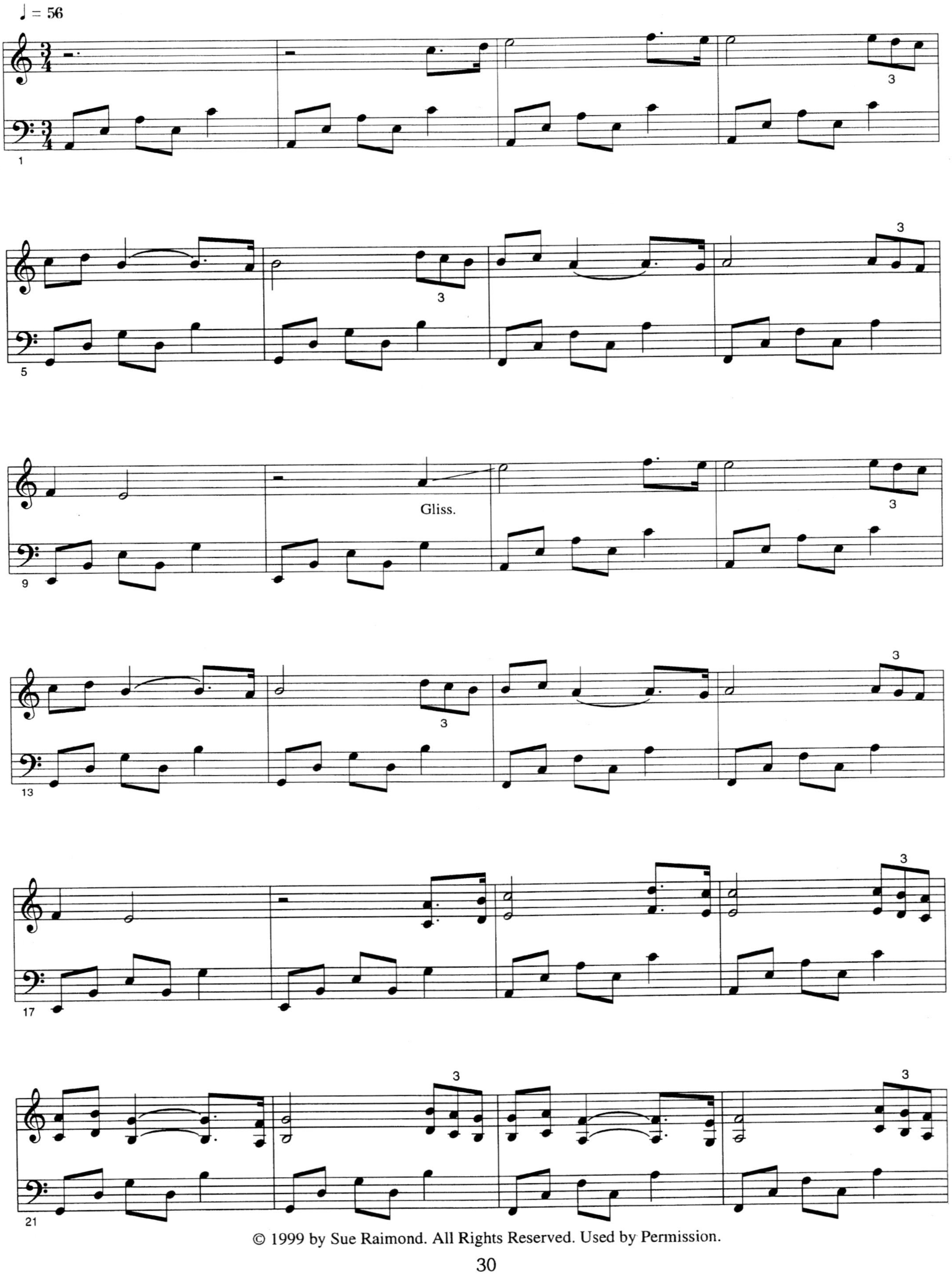

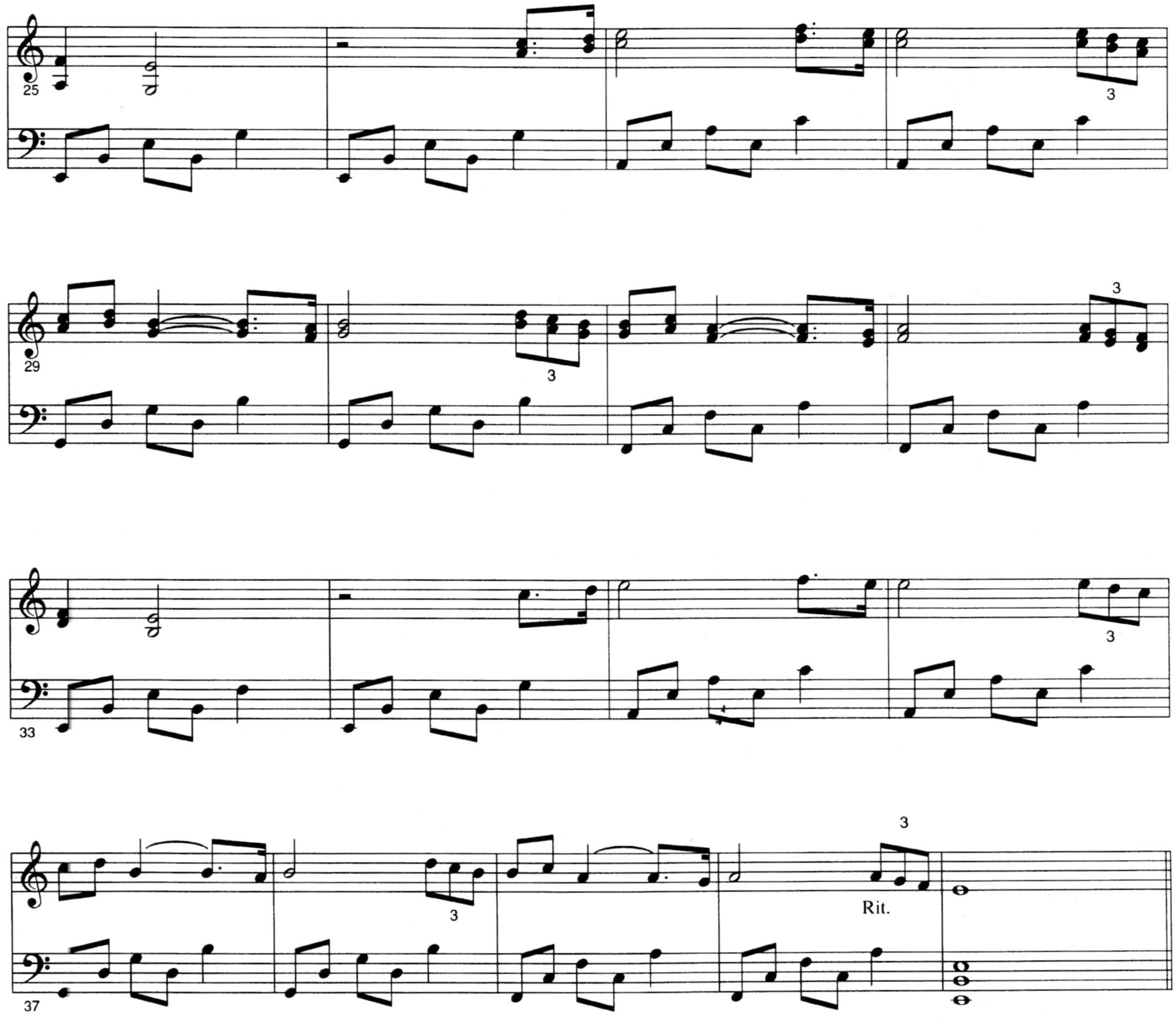
Rit.

*Sue Raimond* is a harper in the ancient tradition of masters whose playing touches the emotions ofthe listener directly — the magical instrument of legend. Simple and deeply moving are the words that come first to mind.

Selections range from light-hearted to haunting, evoking the range of human emotional experience. Her lucid, clear arrangements are perfect for the beginning harper's understanding of the heart of the music — as well as serving as melodic springboards for improvisation.

This beautiful collection is a perfect basis for performance, as well as instruction.

Don Berry

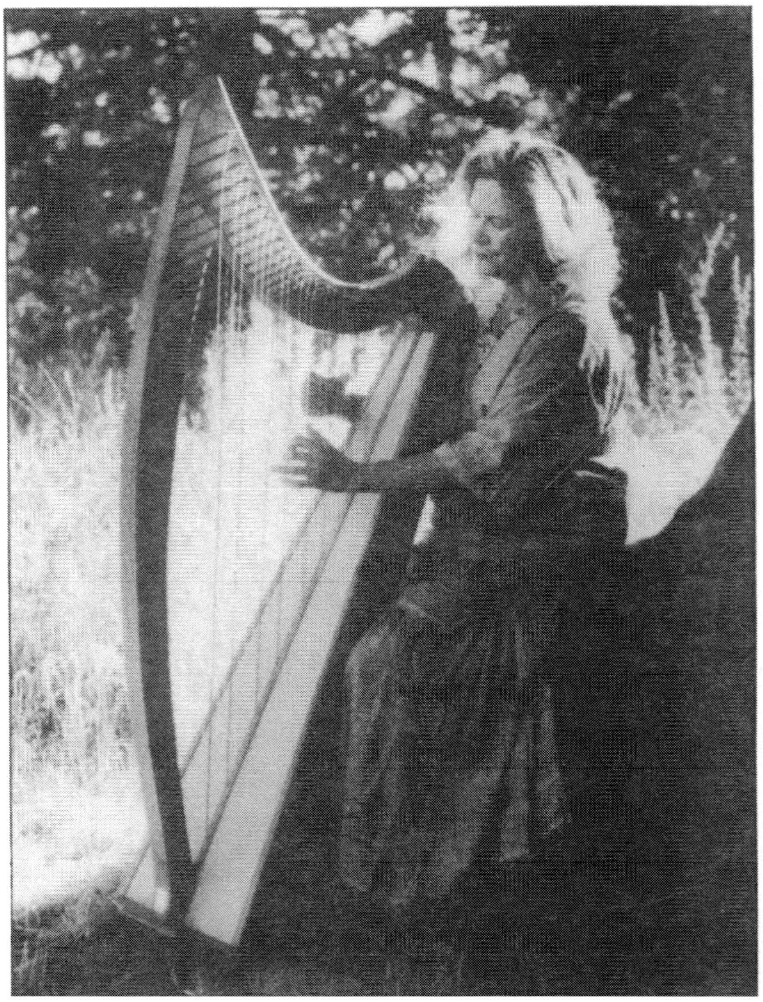

## Music Collections

*Carols and Lullabies • Making Music*

## Sheet Music

*Terwilliger-Widget • Aliso*
*Gentry's Gait • William's Lullaby*
*Matilija • Imagine*

## Recordings

*Carols and Lullabies • Wait for the Sunset*


## Sue Raimond

Sioux Strings
P.O. Box 213, Mt. Laguna, CA 91948
619-473-1213